Tips and Traps
When Renovating
Your Home

Other McGraw-Hill Books by Robert Irwin

Tips and Traps When Renovating Your Home

Robert Irwin

McGraw-Hill

New York   San Francisco   Washington, D.C.   Auckland   Bogotá
Caracas   Lisbon   London   Madrid   Mexico City   Milan
Montreal   New Delhi   San Juan   Singapore
Sydney   Tokyo   Toronto

McGraw-Hill

A Division of The **McGraw·Hill** Companies

1 2 3 4 5 6 7 8 9 0   DOC/DOC   9 0 9 8 7 6 5 4 3 2 1 0 9

ISBN 0-07-134793-3

It was set in Baskerville per the BSF TTS design by Joanne Morbit of the Professional Book Group's composition unit, Hightstown, N.J.

Printed and bound by R. R. Donnelley & Sons Company.

McGraw-Hill books are available at special quantity discounts to use as premiums and sales promotions, or for use in corporate training programs. For more information, please write to the Director of Special Sales, McGraw-Hill, 11 West 19th Street, New York, NY 10011. Or contact your local bookstore.

This book contains the author's opinions. Some material in this book may be affected by changes in the law (or changes in interpretations of the law) or changes in the market conditions since the manuscript was prepared. Therefore, the accuracy and completeness of the information contained in this book and the opinions based on it cannot be guaranteed. Neither the author nor the publisher is engaged in rendering investment, legal, tax, accounting, or other similar professional services. If these services are required, the reader should obtain them from a competent professional.

This book is printed on recycled, acid-free paper containing a minimum of 50% recycled, de-inked fiber.

Contents

Preface

I was recently in a home where the owners were renovating a bathroom. They pointed excitedly to the granite countertop, the whirlpool bath, the gold-plated faucet, and the other truly wonderful features such as a steam towel warmer. Then one said, "When we sell this place, just imagine how much money we'll make!"

So I tried doing just that. They had a modest home and their improvements far and away exceeded the neighborhood's norms. No way could I imagine any buyer paying them back anything close to what it cost them to renovate, not in their neighborhood. They would receive only a fraction of each dollar they spent. Unfortunately, the house was a white elephant—overrenovated.

If they were the exception, I would have just sadly shook my head at the oddity. But, from the great number of home renovations I've seen, I suspect they are more the rule. Most people either over- or underrenovate their homes. Very few have the keen insight to know just how much to put in, in order to get the most back.

Of course, some people point out that renovation is done to please the renovator, hence who cares about the money recouped on sale. Yet, just as I've never met a poker player who liked to lose, I've never met a renovator who liked to lose money on a project. Yes, it's definitely to enjoy the results that most of us remodel, but a home is usually our biggest investment and very few of us can afford to overlook the money side of renovating.

And that's the genesis of this book. I wanted to create a guide that would truly explain how the money works in renovation projects—how to realistically determine the amount you'll get back from your renovation project without resorting to overly simplified charts found elsewhere.

More than that, having built homes from the ground up as well as having done dozens of renovations myself, I wanted to point out the many tips and traps that could benefit readers in the related areas of how to handle contractors and contracts, get accurate bids, work with plans and permissions, and even how to do the projects entirely yourself.

The result is this comprehensive guide to home renovating. It shows you the pitfalls you could trip into when dealing with material suppliers, workers, architects, contractors, and even yourself when you do the work on your own. It goes on to show you how to do projects like a pro giving a multitude of tips on how to save money, time, patience, your health, and even your emotional stability.

From selecting projects that will return the most money to identifying which jobs should be avoided to going through all the steps in the right order to get the best looking and least expensive result, this book will show you the way to a better, cost-saving, profit-producing renovation.

Robert Irwin

Tips and Traps When Renovating Your Home

1

Will I Get My Money Out?

The first and biggest question that anyone usually asks when renovating a home is, "How much money will I get back from the renovation work I do?"

While most of us renovate primarily to make our home more comfortable to live in, only a fool would do the work without an eye to how much value it's adding to the property. Thus, even if you have no intention of reselling in the near future, you will still want to know that, should you sell, you'll get your money back (or at least a sizable portion of it).

TIP

Your home is probably the biggest investment you'll ever make. Protect it by renovating wisely. If you put money into the home that you can't recoup, you're whittling away at your investment—you'll get less cash than you anticipate when you resell.

The last thing you want to do is to sink money into a project with no hope of recouping it. Few projects will return you at least dollar for dollar, but that should be your goal. If it looks like the project will return less than dollar for dollar, it's a good idea to figure out how much less. If it's a lot less, you might decide to skip the renovation project entirely!

TRAP

Will you sell your home soon? Most of us don't really look too far into the future. We're convinced that we'll remain in our current house for many years to come. But statistically, most families move every seven to nine years. A job change, illness, and a change in family size are just a few of the reasons. While you may not currently be planning to move, you may be surprised to find yourself selling your home much sooner than you thought.

But how do you know, in advance, what you'll be able to recoup from the renovation project? How can you determine which projects make financial sense? Will you get more back from renovating a kitchen than a bathroom? What about adding a new front door versus a new skylight? Or an additional bedroom versus a family room?

We all want simple answers, but beware of them in these circumstances. The true answers are tied into such things as the price range of the house, the norms of the neighborhood, and the age of the home as well as how well the renovation turns out.

TRAP

Beware of magazine articles that give quick and simple answers to questions of how much you can recoup: "You'll get 94 percent for a whole kitchen renovation in the West, 83 percent in the South," and so on. Don't believe it for a minute. There are too many factors to consider to offer such a clear-cut solution, and every case is different.

You always have to ask yourself, "Where is the line that separates a renovation that makes financial sense from one that leads to a money pit? Which projects are economically justified and which will price my home out of contention when I go to resell?"

Unfortunately, there is no time-honored rule of thumb that can easily give you a quick answer. There's no simple solution to which renovation project makes sense and which project is "over the top." Remember that what's popular today may be unpopular tomorrow (and could be back in fashion a decade from now). There are renovators who are surprised (and sometimes dismayed) to find that what they thought would add value to their property only turns it into a white elephant. What was tasteful to them turns out to be out of fashion to others.

All of this, however, doesn't mean that there is no way to determine which projects make sense and which don't. You can come up with sensible projects by doing a bit of homework. There are five questions that I always ask myself that help me to decide whether a project is worth doing or not.

TIP

When trying to sort out good projects from bad, always assume that you'll sell your home within a year. No, of course you probably won't, but this gives you a realistic time line for determining how much the project adds to the value of your home. Longer than a year and you run the risk of inflation adding value and thus covering up a possible loss from the project.

The Five Most Important Questions to Ask

1. Is the price range of my home modest, average, or upscale?

2. What are the neighborhood norms?

3. What is the age of my house?

4. What is the market like?

5. What is the ratio of home value to renovation cost?

Is the Price Range of My Home Modest, Average, or Upscale?

Homes come in all price ranges. But if you divide them into three categories—modest, average, and upscale—you very quickly find that certain features are expected for each category.

For example, in a modest-priced home a laminate countertop might be perfectly acceptable. In an upscale home, however, only a granite countertop might do. Laminate might be considered unacceptable.

In an average-priced home, a tiled entryway might be acceptable. In a modest-priced home, however, that might be too costly to consider. And in an upscale home, anything less than a marble entryway might be considered unacceptable.

You want to determine whether your home is modestly priced, average priced, or upscale and renovate to the quality expected. Overrenovate to a quality higher than the price range justifies and you won't get your money out. Underrenovate and you could actually lower the value of the home!

What Is the Norm for the Neighborhood?

You don't want your home to be radically different in size, style, or features from other homes in your neighborhood. You want your home to fit the neighborhood, not stand out like a sore thumb.

If your home, for whatever reason, is below the prevailing neighborhood norms, then bringing it up to par will yield you a good return. The reason, quite simply, is that a subpar house will bring a reduced value anytime you try to resell. Bring that house up to par and you automatically raise its value to neighborhood norms. On the other hand, going beyond the norms of the neighborhood is, again, overrenovating. You won't get your money back.

For example, if all the homes in the neighborhood have two bathrooms and yours has one, spending $20,000 for another bathroom should pay for itself.

On the other hand, if all the homes in your area are 1500 square feet and you spend $50,000 making yours 2000 square feet, you simply won't get your money back. You will have exceeded the neighborhood norms.

I once was asked to sell a renovated, two-story home in a neighborhood where all the surrounding homes were single story. Yes, the renovation nearly doubled the space in the home, and the job was done very well. But buyers didn't want to pay the money the sellers were asking for the larger home because the neighborhood didn't justify it. (For the higher price, buyers would rather move to a better neighborhood!) The sellers never could recoup the money they had spent.

TRAP

Beware of white elephant syndrome. Never overimprove the home for the neighborhood. If you're in a $150,000 neighborhood and do a $25,000 kitchen renovation, chances are you won't get very much of your money back. On the other hand, if you're in a $400,000 neighborhood and do a $25,000 kitchen renovation, you might be underspending! Keep your eye on the big picture, not just the renovation of the moment.

TIP

Ask your neighbors. Yes, you can bring contractors in for estimates, but that tells you only costs, not what the neighborhood norms are. Maybe all the houses in your area have small kitchens and many neighbors have renovated by enlarging their kitchen. The bigger kitchen has become a neighborhood norm, and enlarging your kitchen should fit right in—and allow you to recoup your investment.

What Is the Age of My Home?

Older homes need renovating more than newer homes. If your home is under 10 years old, assuming it was built to the styles of the times, then any heavy renovation you do will probably be overkill.

Your kitchen and bath shouldn't be far out of date. The overall appearance of the home should still be stylish. Spend $15,000 renovating your bathroom and you could literally be spilling the money down the drain.

On the other hand, if your home is over 30 years old and there's been no renovation, then very likely you can get a significant return by updating. This is particularly the case for a full kitchen and bath renovation where the old appliances and format are strikingly out of date. Depending on the neighborhood, you could easily spend $15,000 to $50,000 or more renovating a kitchen and get every penny back, and more.

For homes between 10 and 30 years, it's a toss-up, although partial renovations are more likely to bring a better return. The older the house, the more a major renovation pays. But it's also a function of the market and the neighborhood. Read on.

What about Market Conditions and Location in Recouping My Investment?

It's important to renovate into the prevailing or likely market conditions for your home. If the market is depressed, you'll have trouble recouping your money simply because buyers won't want to spend extra bucks for the work you did. What few buyers there are will be tuned to spending as little as possible.

On the other hand, if the market is hot, you should be able to get more for your renovation. Buyers will like the idea of getting a renovated property and will be willing to pay more for it. They will be able to see themselves reselling for even more money down the road.

TIP

Renovating into a hot market helps you recoup your investment. Renovating into a depressed market makes it more difficult to get your money out.

Another factor is the area of the country you are in. Adding a basement room on the West Coast would be foolish and might net you only a 10 percent return. Not only wouldn't you get your money out, you might actually lower the value of your home! Adding a swimming pool in the Northeast might have the same bad result.

On the other hand, finishing out a basement on the East Coast could return you 75 percent, and a pool on the West Coast could net you 50 percent. Certain areas of the country demand certain features and resist others. You don't want to do something inappropriate for your area.

Further, certain kinds of features are greatly admired in some areas. For example, hardwood floors in the Northeast and Northwest are considered a quality item and are valued. In the Southwest, however, wall-to-wall carpeting is considered standard fare and hardwood floors, though far more expensive to put in, likely won't add any additional value to the property.

What's the Ratio of Home Value to Renovation Cost?

Home values and the costs of renovating differ across the country. It is the ratio between the two that is important. For example, it may cost $25,000 to renovate a kitchen in a home that is worth $200,000 in the South. In this case, the renovation amounts to 12.5 percent of the home's value. On the other hand, a similar home on the West Coast may be valued at $400,000, and the renovation may cost $40,000. Here the renovation is 10 percent of the home's value.

The point is that as a percentage of total value it may cost more to renovate in some areas of the country than others. And the lower a percentage of the home's value it takes to renovate, the more likely you are to recoup your investment.

Five Important Don'ts in Renovating

There are five separate don'ts that you want to avoid. Doing any of these reduces the amount of money you can recoup from your renovation.

Don't Always Try to Save Money by Doing It Yourself

Yes, you can save money, sometimes a lot of money, by doing the job yourself. However, it's important to keep your eye on the doughnut and not the hole. It's not the cost of the job that's critical, but how it turns out.

You may save thousands of dollars by installing a new tile countertop in the bathroom. But if the lines aren't straight, if the grout is too high or too low, if the tiles aren't evenly spaced, the botched job will actually detract from the home. In fact, if you wanted to resell the property at a good price, you might have to call in a professional to rip out your work and redo it!

TRAP

Don't try to save money by skimping on materials. You can ruin a renovation by adding cheap or dated fixtures or by using materials that are drab.

Don't Let Your Personal Tastes Overwhelm Common Sense

Remember, the test is how much more a buyer would pay for the renovation you're going to do. Consequently, you must always keep that potential buyer in mind and try to anticipate what he or she would like.

For example, your favorite color may be hunter green. But is that likely to be the favorite color of a potential buyer? Probably not. In fact, while I myself like hunter green in a home, I recognize that many people find dark colors objectionable.

Thus, you must pick the color, or the renovation project, that is least likely to be considered objectionable, and most likely to be considered desirable. As a result, soothing colors such as beige and white are a good choice. Wood cabinets of currently stylish design, light-colored flooring, and so on are all considered desirable and least likely to offend. On the other hand, deep-sunken tubs, florescent stars painted on a black ceiling, and bathrooms without doors might lower the home's value.

Don't Renovate the Wrong Feature

If your kitchen is old-fashioned, don't choose to renovate the bathroom just because it's less expensive to do. Identify the problem and address it. Yes, it certainly costs more to renovate a kitchen than a bathroom, but in the long run you stand to get all your money out (plus more) from the kitchen renovation because it's needed. On the other hand, you might get very little back from the unneeded bathroom renovation.

Similarly, don't do the kitchen if what the house really needs is more room—add a family room instead. Don't rip out a wall between two rooms that are dark; instead add extra windows or a skylight.

Take the time to identify the problem, then correct it. Don't be sidetracked because the problem is too costly or too difficult. The problem is what it is and doing something else won't help.

Don't Confuse Renovation with Repair

Your cement driveway has cracks, so you spend $5000 putting in a new driveway. Your roof leaks, so you spend $10,000 on a new roof. Your heating system breaks down, so you put in new central heat/air at a cost of $3500. How much have you added to the basic value of your home? The answer? Zero!

You haven't done any renovation. You've only done repair work. All homes need driveways, roofs, and heating units. If yours are in disrepair, then buyers will subtract the cost of repairs from the basic value of the property. If you do the work, then you've just brought the home back to its basic value.

TIP

There is an overlap between renovation and repair. If the kitchen sink leaks and the kitchen countertop tiles are cracked, you need to repair them. But if when doing the work, you add a fancier sink and put in granite countertops, assuming the neighborhood and price range of the home warrant it, you not only have done the repair, but have renovated as well. And you stand to recoup much of your costs.

Don't Get In over Your Head

Calculate the total cost of the renovation you plan *before* you begin any work. Then be sure you have the money to handle it. (See Chapter 5 on financing.)

One of the worst things that can happen is to get halfway through a renovation only to discover that you're short of cash to finish it. In too many cases the owners rip out a kitchen only to discover they can't afford the replacement cabinets. So they have no kitchen, making living in the house virtually impossible. And they can't really sell the place, because few prospective buyers want a home without a kitchen. Then they have trouble refinancing, because most lenders won't loan money on a property where construction is taking place. (See Chapter 8.)

TIP

Don't begin projects you can't finish. Use a sharp pencil to be sure you know how much it's going to cost and where the funds to finish are coming from.

How Much Can You Really Recoup?

All of us want guidelines. They do point us in the right direction, even if their accuracy can sometimes be questioned. Figure 1-1 shows the percentages of investment you can recoup by doing certain projects. Just remember, however, that they are rules of thumb. They are not set in stone. Further, the amounts realized assume that the work needs to be done. For example, all else being equal you can potentially get 110%+ for repainting the front of your house, assuming that the current paint is faded, worn, and dilapidated looking. If the paint is currently in good shape and you just want to repaint to change the color, it's unlikely you'll get anywhere near such a significant return.

Also, to help make the figures more accurate, I've divided them up by the age of the home as well as by the price range. Don't forget to factor in:

By Age of Home

Project

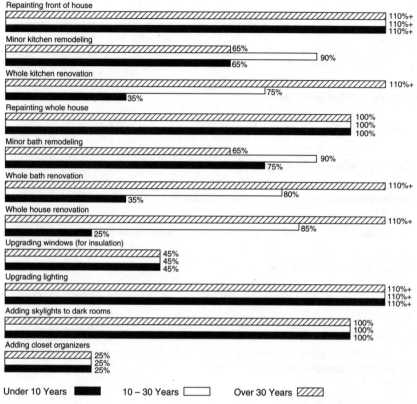

Figure 1-1 How Much of the Cost Can You Recoup?

- Neighborhood norms

- Market conditions

- The area of the country you are in

Note that I've put in "110%+" in cases where you are likely to get more back than you invest. The actual return might be more or slightly less. It depends on many other factors. Thus, I've simply indicated that the return is likely to be very high.

Remember, recouping your investment on any addition is closely linked to the norms of the neighborhood. Further, upscale homes

By Price Range

Project

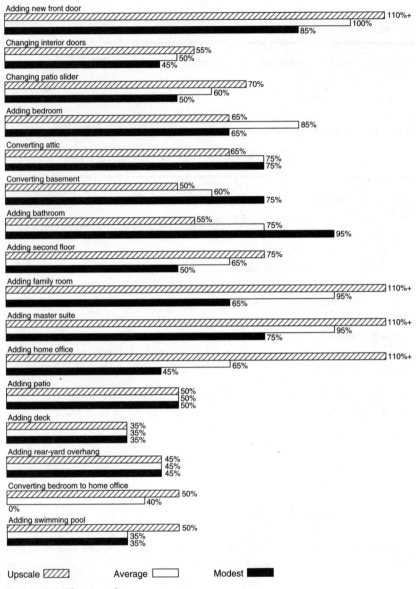

Upscale ▨▨▨   Average ▭   Modest ▬▬

Figure 1-1 (*Continued*)

are already likely to be bigger; hence any addition is less likely to have a dramatic effect. On the other hand, additions to modest homes may be considered overrenovating. Further, upscale homes are usually built with many bathrooms and bedrooms. Adding more might just be overkill.

TIP

You can undoubtedly get your money back faster and easier, plus get a quicker sale (if you are indeed selling), by making cosmetic changes to any home. Paint your house. Add better landscaping. Put on a new front door. These are among the least expensive renovations, and for a few thousand dollars on a relatively new house, they yield the best return.

TRAP

Keep in mind that any renovation you do today may need to be redone in 20 years! You may have lived through the entire value of your investment over that period of time.

2

Which Project First? Creating Priorities

If you're going to do a renovation project, it's helpful to know what you need to do in roughly the order you'll need to do it. Not having this most basic kind of information can delay your project, if not actually derail it.

Your priorities, or the order in which you need to accomplish things and how long each will take, will vary enormously, depending on the project. However, it's possible to get a general idea of what you'll need to do in order to proceed. Figure 2-1 gives a typical time line that lets you see what's to be done, the order in which it should be done, and the time it might take to do it. In later chapters we'll deal with each of the items mentioned in greater detail.

TIP

In most cases, demolition is done first. However, sometimes it can be done later, as when you leave an outside wall intact to protect the building while adding on or when you leave a working sink or toilet in place while renovating a bathroom. Sometimes delaying demolition allows you to utilize or protect the house while the work goes on.

As you can see, the amount of time required will vary enormously. While a small project itself could conceivably be done in little over

15

Preparation	
1. Gather ideas and information	Up to 2 months
2. "Guesstimate" what it might cost (to see if you're even in the ballpark for doing the project)	1 day
3. Line up the money	Up to 3 weeks
4. Get your plans and permissions	1–3 weeks
5. Locate contractors and get bids	1–3 weeks
Actual Project	
6. Take care of demolition	1–2 days
7. Install cabinets	1–2 days
Refinish cabinets	1–4 days
8. Install countertops	1–5 days (depending on type)
9. Install appliances (sink, range, oven, etc.)	1 day
10. Install flooring	1–3 days
11. Install lighting	1–2 days
12. Paint, wallpaper	1–5 days

Figure 2-1 Typical Time Line for Renovating a Kitchen

a week (if everything goes perfectly, as it never does!), it may end up taking a month or more. And the actual time spent—when you add in gathering ideas, getting plans and permissions, locating contractors, getting bids, and so on—can extend to many months.

As you go through this book, you'll see the pitfalls you might run into as well as the ways you can save time and money. But first, use the personal renovation time line in Figure 2-2 to get started with your project.

What Project Should I Do First?

Few people have only one renovation project in mind. Typically they have many and that's only natural. If the kitchen needs redoing, chances are so do the bathrooms. And when it comes to what's needy, there are always the doors, the windows, the flooring, and on and on.

Fill in the blanks to determine the time it will take to finish your renovation project.

Preparation	Time to Accomplish Task
1. Gather ideas and information	_____
2. "Guesstimate" what it might cost (to see if you're even in the ballpark for doing the project)	_____
3. Line up the money	_____
4. Get your plans and permissions	_____
5. Locate contractors and get bids	_____

Actual Project (skip tasks that are inappropriate for your project)

6. Demolition	_____
7. Foundation	_____
8. Framing	_____
9. Roof	_____
10. Flooring	_____
11. Exterior walls/windows	_____
12. Rough plumbing, electrical	_____
13. Rough heating, air ducts	_____
14. Insulation	_____
15. Finish electrical/plumbing/heating	_____
16. Install 1st _____	_____
17. Install 2nd _____	_____
18. Install 3rd _____	_____
19. Install 4th _____	_____
20. Install 5th _____	_____
21. Install 6th _____	_____
22. Install/finish flooring	_____
23. Install/finish lighting	_____
24. Paint and wallpaper; complete other finish work	_____
25. Clean up	_____

Figure 2-2 Project Time Line

If you have unlimited money, you can do it all. If not, you have to pick and choose. Which projects should you do now? And which projects should you hold off until later (when funds to tackle them are available)?

For a typical older house, chances are your list of projects includes the following. (Of course, if your house is newer, you'll have a much shorter list.)

Typical Renovation Projects

Kitchen	Whole or partial renovation
Bathrooms	Whole or partial renovation
Front doors	Replace
Family room	Add or expand
Skylights	Add in dark areas
Windows	Replace with double-pane and/or greenhouse windows
Wood finish	Replace throughout house
Interior doors	Replace and upgrade
Flooring	Replace and renovate
Electrical, plumbing, heating	Repair and upgrade

You want to do it all because you know it all needs doing. However, the total cost might easily be $50,000 or more. It might even be much more if you do all the work at once, since you won't be able to live in the house during renovation.

What you may need to do is prioritize the different projects; decide which is most important and do it first.

How Do I Decide What's Most Important?

What criteria should you use for determining which projects come first? For me, the following three are vital:

1. What affects safety and health?

2. What makes the biggest difference in recouping money?

3. What's going to make the property most livable?

Priority 1: What Affects Safety and Health?

Changes that involve safety and health aren't really renovation, but repair. If your gas furnace has a hole in the heat exchanger, you (or anyone else living in the house) run the danger of carbon monoxide poisoning. The hole needs to be fixed, immediately. It could cost upwards of $2000.

Every home needs to have at least one smoke alarm, preferably several. And they should be both the battery and home electrical circuit variety. The cost is minimal, usually under $25 each.

Perhaps the wiring is frayed in spots, particularly at ceiling fixtures. It must be replaced or repaired. Again, as long as it's bad only in spots, the cost is minimal, usually under $100.

TRAP

Beware of homes, particularly older ones, with obvious and not so obvious building code violations. For example, a bathroom may be right off a kitchen—a definite no-no, because of the potential for mixing unsanitary with sanitary conditions. Or rooms may have been torn out and replaced without the proper studding and headers. Or a staircase may be too narrow. You may have to renovate these defects just to make the home marketable. (Today's home inspections often turn up code violations, and buyers usually demand that they be corrected before completing the purchase.)

Maybe the plumbing is galvanized steel that has rusted out and is leaking. Perhaps the only real solution is to replace everything with copper piping. This is a real bad one in terms of price—figure a minimum of $5000 for the whole house.

TIP

In a pinch you can use compression fittings (found at hardware stores) over leaks to stop them. This will work as a temporarily solution. However, if the galvanized pipe is indeed rusting out, other leaks will soon appear elsewhere.

Is there lead paint in the home? (Most homes built prior to 1978 used lead paint.) Many people are willing to live with lead paint in the house. However, if there are children, it could be a significant health hazard, since kids sometimes chew on paint or ingest dust or dirt that carries lead paint particles. Talk about price! Lead paint can be removed only by experts (who use special protective masks and controlled removal techniques). Figure the cost at $10,000 and up for a whole house!

What about asbestos? It may be on pipes, in acoustical ceilings, in floor tile, and elsewhere. Fortunately, if it's not disturbed, it's usually not a threat. Indeed, one often acceptable method of controlling asbestos is to have it encapsulated. But if it's loose, it needs to be removed, immediately. Again, removal must be handled by specialists, and the cost is very high. Start at $1000 and go on up, depending on the location and quantity to be removed.

The list goes on and on. If you have a pool, is it surrounded by a protective fence up to building code requirements (usually at least 5 feet high)? Are the electrical outlets all properly grounded?

Will I Get My Money Back?   What's important to understand is that doing the above work doesn't earn you any more dollars when it comes time to sell the property. That's because the work is actually a repair. And buyers just won't pay extra for repairs. They figure it's your responsibility to do the work as the owner/seller.

TRAP

Buyers have little imagination. You may have spent thousands on a new furnace, new plumbing, and lead paint removal. However, buyers will simply say to themselves that what you've done is the minimal expected to sell the property and doesn't deserve their paying a higher price. If buyers can't see the renovation, they usually won't pay for it.

Yet you need to do the work. And usually you need to do it at the highest priority, because it affects your health and safety. It won't do you much good to focus on some other work if the house burns down or floods, or if you get sick because you overlooked some pressing health issue. Just don't count on your efforts accomplishing more than bringing the home up to minimal standards.

TIP

 As a home buyer, you should seriously consider how much hidden work needs to be done before making an offer. That's the reason for having a thorough inspection of the property *before* you buy.

Priority 2: What Makes the Biggest Difference in Recouping Money?

The next most important criterion is money. You don't want to spend hard-earned bucks on a project that won't pull its own weight. In Chapter 1 we discussed the likely percentage return on different projects. Take another look and consider giving priority to the projects that return the highest amount on your investment.

Usually this means doing all the cosmetic work first. The return is the corollary to recouping on hidden work. Cosmetic work is the most visible. People can see it, dramatically. Paint the house, put in new carpeting, landscape the front—all the work you do will be readily visible. As a result, you should get back dollar for dollar or more on your investment.

Cosmetic Renovation Guide

Painting	Do the front first, then the inside, then the entire outside.
Wallpapering and paneling	Wallpapering costs more than painting, but when done with taste, it looks richer. Beware of paneling, since it has as many detractors as admirers.
New front door	Costs more than painting the old door, but ends up looking far better.
New garage door	Makes a big difference in enhancing the curb appeal of a home.
New driveway	Repaving or putting in new concrete says the home is quality-built.

Window treatment	Drapes, shutters, and curtains, handled tastefully, add enormously to the home's value.
Flooring	New carpeting and wood or tile floors are expensive, but they boost the quality of the home.
Landscaping	Pay attention to the front. You can let the rear and side go, if you must.

Priority 3: What's Going to Make the Property Most Livable?

Finally, we come down to what you want to do. Yes, it makes the most sense to fix the leaky roof and to paint the house. But you just can't stand the fact that there's no shower in the bathroom—you hate taking tub baths. So you elevate the bathroom renovation to top position.

Don't deny your wants. After all, unless you're renovating simply to make money by quickly reselling (a possibility), you're going to be living in the renovated home. If you don't like what you're living in, it will affect your temperament, your efficiency, and even your health.

TIP

If you're going to live in the home for a long time, you may want to consider projects that reduce your living expenses. These include double-pane windows, insulation at doors, new insulation in the attic, a more efficient water heater and furnace, and so forth. Just keep in mind, however, that most of these projects are not visible, so you won't get much of your investment back.

To my way of thinking, unless you've got some killer feature that you just can't stand, personal livability should be the last priority. Yes, it certainly is important, but it should come after safety and recouping your money.

One livability project that many people overlook is increasing storage space. Many homes simply don't have enough closet room. Adding a clothes organizer to a closet can be a big help both to you and to the value of your home.

TRAP

 Beware of combining two small bedrooms into one larger one with bigger closet space. Most people would prefer to have more bedrooms, even if they are tiny. Instead, consider expanding storage into the garage or laundry room, or even adding on externally.

A friend of mine once decided to renovate the kitchen in his older home. He simply couldn't stand the way it looked. So he ripped out the countertop, sink, and cabinets. While he was at it, he decided to tackle the main bathroom too. So he ripped out the sink, toilet, and tub. And as long as the house was a thorough mess, he decided to go ahead and combine a small dining room and kitchen eating area into one larger family room. Naturally he tore apart both rooms.

After several weeks, the home was in a state of demolition: unlivable. Then my friend decided to get started rebuilding. Of course, at that point he had done so much work that completing the renovation project would take months—if he had the money, which it turned out he was far short on. He had to move out and eventually lost the house in foreclosure!

The moral here is tackle one project at a time; finish it before starting the next. You'll get more done, do it quicker, and sleep better at night.

3

Collecting Ideas and Information

The worst thing you can do when renovating is try to reinvent the wheel. Regardless of how big or small your renovation project, don't think that you're the first person to ever attempt it. You're not. While there may be some new twists peculiar to your home, in general everything that can be done in renovation has been done by others. Benefit from their experience.

There are a host of resources available to you before you start your project. Take a look at these and "steal" ideas from them. You may want to put a Jacuzzi® in your bathroom. See how others have done it—the layout they used, how they made it fit into a small space—and check the different styles, colors, and prices available. Or you may want to renovate your entire home. Check out what others have done with a home similar to yours—the clever cost-cutting tricks they used, how they made use of space and light. Look into your options.

Your resources today are almost limitless.

What about Magazines and Books?

There are a host of magazines out there that cater to renovators. Many are composed entirely of plans for home design. Others concentrate on kitchen and bath. Still others emphasize interior design. Never mind the furniture in the photos—look at the rooms the furniture is in for new ideas! Here is a partial list:

American Style Mostly about furniture and colors, but check out the photos of rooms for ideas.

Bedrooms and Baths   Mostly on decorating, but you'll get lots of ideas on different looks for rooms, some you may like.

Home   Check out the ads. You might find just the faucet or toilet bowl you're looking for. Also, good for ideas on converting space.

Home and Architectural Trends   A great dream book. You'll get all kinds of fantastic ideas, but most may be too expensive for your pocketbook.

Homestyles Home Plans   A few articles on design, but mostly different style homes with whole-house layouts. Blueprints available for a fee.

Interior Design   Mostly on commercial buildings, but some articles on dream homes.

Taunton's Fine Home Building   Great ideas and tips on new building techniques, from countertops to rain gutters.

This Old House   Like the television show, only broader in scope. Covers the field from landscaping to porches.

These magazines should all be available (or can be ordered) at your local magazine stand or bookstore. You don't need to subscribe to or buy all these publications (although you may want a subscription to one or two that seem particularly attuned to your needs). But you will find it helpful to peruse several of them. Sometimes just looking at the pictures will give you a new idea, something you hadn't considered, for solving a design problem.

TRAP

Be careful of using the plans acquired from magazines and mail-order promotions just as they are. While some may be quite complete, you usually will need to take them to an architect or draftsperson to have them redrawn to your needs.

TIP

A home renovation will never come out looking the same as the picture in the magazine. Yours will look different, perhaps better in your eyes. You're just there to get ideas, not to try to replicate what you see.

Should I Try Showrooms?

Every manufacturer of a home product has a showroom somewhere. Some showrooms feature one manufacturer's products. Others display the products of many different manufacturers in groups, such as kitchens or baths. The showrooms are another great place to get ideas for what you want to do in your renovation.

The Whole House

Believe or not, there are whole-house showrooms. These are the model homes that builders offer. If you're about to undertake a whole-house renovation, stop! Don't do another thing until you check out the model homes in your area. You will very quickly learn what's currently in style (what buyers are looking for). You may find that you want to adopt many of the new features that builders offer.

Also, check out any resales that are of similar design and age as your home, particularly if they are located in your neighborhood. In most cases, you will be able to see them by going to "open houses." In other cases, a friendly real estate agent will be happy to take you by.

TIP

You needn't use a subterfuge to get the agent to show you homes—you don't have to say you're really a buyer when you're not. Just explain that you're renovating your home and that when you're done, you'll consider reselling. That's only the truth. An agent will be delighted to show you homes in the hopes of eventually getting a listing on yours—and possibly selling you another one.

Kitchens and Baths

Home centers such as Home Depot, Home Base, Orchard Supply, and others have showrooms for kitchen and bath. Many retailers that specialize in kitchen and bath fixtures also have extensive showrooms. The same is true of cabinet manufacturers.

Your best bet is to check the Yellow Pages of your phone book. Look for ads under the following headings:

Bathroom cabinets and equipment

Bathtubs

Cabinets

Kitchen cabinets and equipment

Kitchen/bathroom remodeling

Pay particular attention to advertising that says, "Visit our show-room." I suggest you call first to be sure that the showroom is open (not itself being renovated!) and has enough variety to be of interest to you.

Fixtures

Retailers specialize in a variety of home fixtures, from appliances such as stoves and ovens to lighting fixtures and faucets. These retailers also have their own showrooms.

While visiting a fixture showroom is always useful, it's a necessity when you get down to the nitty-gritty of assembling the materials for your renovation. The reason is that you'll get an idea of what's out there and, just as important, how much it costs. For example, you may think you can get a good-looking faucet assembly for your bath-room sink and tub at a price of under $100 (for both).

While you can get them for that price, their appearance is likely to be plain and the materials used may be cheap. Actually, a first-class faucet for a bathroom sink will cost $150 or more. A first-class Roman style faucet for a spa tub could easily cost $500 and up. And that's just for the faucet! High-quality lighting fixtures also can be expensive. Then there's the cost of the sinks and tubs, and we're only in the bathroom!

Visiting fixture showrooms will give you a realistic handle on what's available, what it costs, and even how long it takes to order.

What Are My Internet Options?

These days any business that's worth its salt has a Web site. (Check out robertirwin.com, by the way!) That includes manufacturers of virtually any product you'll need in your home renovation—from cabinet makers to flooring manufacturers. Many local contractors also have their own Web sites. Visiting these sites will give you a glimpse of the newest products, provide information on cost, installation, and delivery, and fill you with a host of new ideas. Here are just a few of my favorite sites.

www.yahoo.com, www.excite.com, and www.lycos.com. Generic search engines. The following search words are helpful:

home or remodeling

home shows

home design

kitchen and bathroom

www.buildingonline.com and www.build.com Search engines with links to many manufacturers of home consumer products, including sinks and cabinets, as well as to contractors, associations, and architects.

www.taunton.com Taunton Press books, tapes, and videos on virtually every area of home improvement, with emphasis on doing it yourself.

www.kohler.com An online showroom for Kohler's wide range of sinks and kitchen and bath fixtures and faucets.

www.faucet.com An online showroom for faucets and other fixtures. Offers some discounted merchandise.

www.diamond2.com Pictures of different cabinet styles and designs from Diamond Cabinets, a national distributor.

www.kraftmaid.com Maker of high-quality kitchen cabinets.

www.merilat.com Manufacturer of cabinets sold nationwide.

www.daltile.com Manufacturers of a wide variety of tiles used in kitchens, baths, entryways, and elsewhere.

www.thisoldhouse.com The original home remodeling show from public television. It goes through a complete home renovation. Site contains info on many of the previous shows as well as the homes that were done and lists contractors and manufacturers.

www.homeimprovement.com The Web site for the *HomeTime* show seen both on public television and the Learning Channel. Includes tips from the shows on virtually every aspect of home renovation. Sells videos and books.

www.nari.org The Web site for the National Association of the Remodeling Industry. Contains many references to other sites as well as good tips on selecting contractors and on doing the work yourself, including coming up with a workable design.

What's Available on TV?

I'm sure you've already seen many of them, but within the last few years dozens of truly excellent home renovation shows have emerged on PBS, TLC, and other networks—from *This Old House* to *HomeTime* to many more. Don't overlook the opportunity these shows offer. They are great for getting ideas as well as for seeing how things are done. While many of the shows gloss over the real how-to aspects of jobs, some go into scrupulous detail.

Of course, you can't be watching TV all the time, and chances are the shows won't be demonstrating the very project you want to do, just when you want to do it. So check out their Web sites. Several are given above. You can usually buy tapes by specific show as well by category of project (kitchen, bath, windows, doors, etc.).

What about Checking with Designers and Architects?

It really depends on how big a project you have in mind and how thick your wallet is.

Architects can give you ideas, but they are in business to create plans and designs, so you may have to pay for them. Typically, architects will want some sort of upfront fee, to ensure that you are really serious about doing the work. Then, they will talk with you, point out design ideas in books and magazines, and show you plans and sketches of their earlier projects. When they have a good idea of what you want, they'll usually make sketches. You can see how these look and then make adjustments or changes. When everything is just as you like, they'll draw up a set of plans that any competent builder can execute.

The cost is high, but the results are usually worth it. If it's a whole house, the architect may want a percentage of the overall building costs. For smaller projects there may be a set fee or a per hour charge. Figure on spending at least $1000 and often considerably more for architectural services.

Designers work a little differently. Often they get some or all of their fee from the manufacturers of products that you buy. However, in some cases they too may want an upfront fee (sometimes refundable after you make purchases) or an hourly fee.

Designers can take you to local "design centers"—large showrooms (sometimes covering an entire building) where manufacturers are set up to display everything from furniture to window treatments to kitchen appliances. Some designers may be able to save you considerable money by getting products at steep discounts and passing some of that savings along to you. Usually, however, they deal only in the better-quality items, so the prices are pretty steep to begin with.

Designers are listed in the Yellow Pages under interior design. However, you're better off if you can get a recommendation from a friend who has worked successfully with one. Builders, showroom salespeople, and furniture salespeople can also recommend designers.

4

"Guesstimating" How Much It Will Cost

The real title of this chapter should be "How Much Can I Afford?" But, at least at the beginning, few of us really want to think about what we can afford. Instead, we want to get a rough sense of what it's going to cost. Only then will we worry about whether we can afford it and *if* we want to proceed!

For example, we may feel we need to do a complete kitchen makeover. Our cabinets are old and dilapidated, the countertop tile is cracked, the cuts in the linoleum floor are accumulating dirt, the lighting is inadequate. In short, we need a new, renovated kitchen. What will it cost?

If it costs $5000, maybe we'll start tomorrow. If it costs $10,000 to $15,000, we'll think about it. If it costs $50,000, we'll probably say forget it, or at least think about using a less expensive approach.

TIP

At the beginning there's usually a big spread between what it's going to cost and what we anticipate we can afford to spend. Most people are shocked to find out how high true renovation costs are. As a result, budgets tend to start small and grow big. However, you can do it the other way too. You can start with a big project and then whittle it down to your budget's size. It's all a matter of guesstimating.

In Chapter 9, we'll look at ways to get highly accurate bids from contractors and suppliers of materials. But we're not at that stage yet. Here, we are more interested in a very rough estimate of how much a project will cost so that we can see if it's in the ballpark and therefore if we really want to do anything at all.

Five Steps to a Guesstimate

Guesstimates can be obtained in a five-step process:

1. Get ballpark bids from contractors.
2. Check out materials costs at retailers.
3. Add in a cost for demolition and cleanup.
4. Add in an allowance for changes you'll want to make.
5. Add 10 percent more for the unforeseen.

Get Ballpark Bids from Contractors

Almost any contractor is willing to come out, take a look at the job, and give you a bid. The only question is: How accurate will that bid be?

TIP

To get an accurate bid from a contractor, you need to have a set of plans, a list of specs (an indication of the materials you want), and a timetable for completion. If you don't have all that, you're just getting a ballpark figure.

At an early stage of the game, chances are that the contractor will make a high bid, figuring that you do not really know what you want and will change your requirements over time. The contractor has to build in protection in case you end up wanting something substantially different from what you are now asking for. Often a contractor's bid will include a variety of options. Here's a typical ballpark bid for an upgraded kitchen:

Complete Kitchen Cabinets, Installed

All new cabinets, in stained wood	$11,400
All new cabinets in plastic white	$7,300
All new cabinets with glass doors	$12,200
Existing cabinets with new doors and veneer	$6,100
Existing cabinets sanded and restained	$4,200

Since you don't know what you want, the contractor is offering you a variety of options to choose from. Of course, each option is still a guesstimate, probably high, of what it will really cost. You have to sit down and pick out the specific cabinets, the stain you want, the configuration, whether you want to buy new or refinish old, and so on. Obviously, the choices you make will dramatically influence the cost. Nevertheless, the contractor's initial bids here can help you see relative costs and what it will take to do the job with different types of materials.

How do you find contractors to give you guesstimates? Ask friends who are pleased with the work they had done. Ask real estate agents. Look for cabinet shops, tilers, kitchen specialists, and so on in the phone book.

Call several. Ask them to come by for an evaluation. Most contractors will do this for free. Typically they will stop by and spend around an hour with you. They'll give you options, possibly with a quick sketch of what they plan to do, and supply a ballpark estimate of costs.

Also check out contractors who specialize in remodeling jobs. They'll come out and look at your overall job, suggest options, perhaps come up with a brief plan, and give you a variety of costs depending on the options you choose.

Check Out Materials Costs

Next, check with local building supply stores. Companies from Home Depot to small emporiums that sell cabinets, countertops, and flooring will often offer a design service. For a small fee, usually around $50, their representatives will come out to your home and take accurate measurements, even photos. Then back at the store they'll run a computer program to show you how things will look with items you picked at the showroom as well as give you a rough breakdown of costs.

Check with manufacturers. Again at building supply stores as well as distributors that work with the public (tile showrooms, cabinet makers, and so on) you can get prices on materials only. Often these sources will tell you what you need to complete the job yourself and give you a surprisingly accurate estimate of materials costs. If you're a do-it-yourselfer, this is a great place to start. It's also a very good way to check out installation costs. (*Don't forget:* To the cost of materials, you need to add the cost of having someone do the installation.)

TIP

 When you're looking at materials, be sure you get all the extras. For example, a kitchen sink may cost $250. In addition, you may want a new faucet assembly, which can cost another $150. Then there's the connecting pipes and materials—say, another $50. Finally, a new sink usually needs a new garbage disposal, for another $100. Thus, your sink in reality, with extras, costs $550 uninstalled. Get the real cost, not just the stripped-down cost without the necessary extras.

Add In a Cost for Demolition and Cleanup

A contractor will automatically add in the cost of demolishing your existing kitchen, bath, or whatever you want to renovate as well as a cost of removing the debris after demolition and cleaning up after the job is done.

If you're trying to figure out actual costs, however, you'll need to add in a figure here. In a typical renovation project not involving saving the materials, the costs needn't be much, usually several hundreds dollars—often under $300 if the project involves just one or two rooms. On the other hand, if you're dealing with an old home with fancy wood trim that's costly to replicate, you may want to save what you take out. That can be time-consuming and very expensive.

A regular demolition without saving what you're tearing out does not require the services of a specialist. If you want to save a few bucks, you can do it yourself. Otherwise, you can hire a laborer to come in and do the work for you.

Cleanup is dusty and dirty and can involve hauling away heavy old materials. Again, you can do it yourself to save a few bucks or pay someone to haul it away.

TIP

If you want to do the demolition yourself, fine. You can take out a lot of anger and frustration banging on walls and countertops. (Just be sure to wear goggles and protective clothing so that you don't get injured.) But cleanup is no fun. I suggest you pay the small amount it costs to have someone else do it.

Add In an Allowance for Changes

Do you know exactly what you want done right now? Chances are pretty slim that you'll answer yes. At this point, you're embarking more on an information-gathering mission. Hence changes are the rule.

However, it would be a mistake to think that you'll really ever be completely satisfied with what you plan to do. I recall the story of a famous artist whose paintings still hang in the Louvre in Paris. Every month or so (going back several decades) he would stop by to admire them. However, upon taking a closer look, he would inevitably decide that something wasn't quite the way he wanted it. So, surreptitiously, he'd take out his paints and touch up the paintings. His work was never done.

So even though you may have a plan and a series of specifications indicating exactly the materials you want, don't count on not changing your mind. More likely, as you begin work you will decide that you want a different cabinet, color, layout, or whatever.

It happens. Prepare for it. Set aside an allowance for changes.

TRAP

The most expensive costs are those involving changing a plan. It means the contractor has to do additional work, often involving removing work already completed. Since the changes aren't in the original bid, they are usually added on a time-plus-materials basis, the costliest way to go. Keep your changes to a minimum and you'll save loads of money.

How much do you set aside? It depends on how fickle you are. If you tend to change your mind frequently and can never decide on what you want, then I'd set aside a hefty allowance—perhaps as much as 30 percent of the total costs or more!

On the other hand, if you're the sort who sticks by a decision once made, then you may want to add only 5 percent. Chances are once you've got a set of plans and specifications, you won't want to change much.

TIP

You'll always find something you want to do differently. Unless you're very experienced, you won't be able to visualize how a project will come out from the plans and specs. Rather, you'll need to see it completed to realize what it will look like. And inevitably there will be something you find you must have different. Even if you normally never change your mind once you set it, add in a small allowance for changes. You'll find you'll use it up.

Add 10 Percent More for the Unforeseen

Finally, you'll want to add an amount to cover totally unforeseen events. The contractor could break into a wall only to discover that there's a lot of plumbing behind it, requiring the costly services of a plumber. Or, in the process of adding a garden window, you learn the model you were counting on has just been discontinued and you can only get a different, far more expensive window. Or you find that although you planned on living in the house during the renovation, you simply can't stand the dust and mess and decide to move to a motel for a week.

Expect the unexpected. If you do, you won't be unprepared when it occurs. My suggestion is that you add in 10 percent of the total cost here.

As shown in Figure 4-1, when all is said and done, the general contractor's initial guesstimate often is not much higher than the costs of materials and installation of individual parts when you act as the general contractor. This is frequently because the general contractor can get deals that you can't. Indeed, many general contractors who specialize in remodeling are actually cabinet makers, tilers, and so on, so their cost of materials is very low. Also, they hire installers on a regular basis and may get lower prices. It's something to consider if you're thinking about saving money and doing the contracting work yourself.

Again, you *can* save money by doing it yourself. In the example in Figure 4-1, at least $5000 is attributed to installer's costs. Do it yourself and you'll save this amount. However, keep in mind that the cost for installation in this example is less than 20 percent of the total cost. You won't really save that much. (Where you can save big is if you do any electrical and plumbing work yourself.)

Also note that the charges for changes and for the unexpected must be added to both the materials costs and the general contractor's costs.

1. General contractor's estimate to put in new cabinets, countertop, flooring, and lights		$21,000
2. Materials-only costs (with installation)		
Cabinets	$8,500	
Countertop	4,500	
Flooring	1,500	
Lighting	600	
Installation	5,000	
3. Demolition and cleanup	500	
4. Changes you'll want to make	5,000	5,000
5. 10 percent for the unforeseen	2,500	2,500
	$28,100	$28,500

Figure 4-1 Typical Guesstimate of Costs for a Kitchen Renovation

(Costs for demolition and cleanup are, presumably, already accounted for by the contractor.)

How Do I Make a Go-Ahead Decision?

Once you get rough costs, you'll have some idea of what your first project will entail. There may be an enormous range of prices. For example, your kitchen project could range from $6000—if you just restain the cabinets, put inexpensive tile on the countertop and linoleum on the floor, and do it yourself—to $40,000 for new cabinets, a stone countertop, and a wood floor, all done professionally.

Now it's time to bite the bullet and make your first reversible decision. (I call it reversible because you're still guesstimating.) You don't know exactly what all the expenses will be, although you have ballpark figures. So you can stand back and ask yourself, "Can I afford that?"

TIP

 You're at the "what if" stage. When you're just getting started, nothing's written in stone. You're just trying out different ideas, costs, and results to see how they feel. You're not committed in any way to follow through on any of it. That's why it's very important to be open and to entertain as many alternatives as possible.

However, from the priorities we discussed earlier, you should now have a clearer sense of what the project will cost. Your next question likely is, "How do I pay for it?"

We'll cover that topic in the next chapter.

5
Can I
Finance It?

Whether your renovation project involves putting in a new $200 sink or $50,000 kitchen, at some point labor and materials people are going to stick out their hands and say, "Pay me!"

In almost all cases the supplier will want cash (unless it is a large company that handles its own financing, rare in this field). So now you must find a way to come up with the money.

TIP

Typically you'll need to pay a portion of the renovation cost up front when the job starts and then the balance when it's finished. For big jobs, midpoint payments may also be required.

As you begin figuring out where to get the money, the most important mistake to avoid is to think piecemeal. You should always attempt to arrange for the maximum amount of funds you will need. If you estimate your project is going to cost $10,000, then get financing for the entire amount. (Actually, arrange for $11,000, just to be sure!)

TRAP

Never, ever, start any renovation project unless you have arranged for *all* the financing. Be sure you know exactly where the money is coming from to complete the job *before* you begin. The last thing you want to do is to find yourself halfway through the project without enough money to finish. You could end up with a ripped-apart home that you might not be able to live in, might not be able to sell, and (if things go really badly) might even lose to foreclosure!

Can I Really Afford to Do It?

My mother used to tell me, "Don't have eyes bigger than your stomach!" She was cautioning me not to waste food, to take only as much as I could eat—good advice for anyone.

A similar approach applies when renovating. Never tackle a project that you can't really afford. Yes, a new $25,000 bathroom will add enormously to the livability of your home. And eventually, when you decide to sell, it will add value and salability. But if you can't afford to spend $25,000, it doesn't matter. You shouldn't tackle the project.

TIP

An exception here is if you're renovating in order to resell quickly (which most people aren't). Here, you must create a sales plan that incorporates all the costs of renovation (including finance interest and sales expenses), plus your profit, to be recouped from the sale. Even so, you're walking a fine time line—if you don't sell quickly enough, the renovation costs could cause you to lose big time.

So how do you know if you can afford it? Most of us think we have an accurate feeling for what we can and can't afford. We can afford a Chevy or maybe a Toyota. But a Lincoln or a Rolls Royce is out of our reach.

Maybe so, and then again maybe not. My own experience in dealing with hundreds of real estate borrowers is that often people either exaggerate or minimalize what they actually can afford. It may turn out that you really can afford more, or less, than you think.

To help you analyze your actual financing situation a little better, take the quiz in Figure 5-1. See how you score. If you're still unsure about how much you can afford, consider checking with a financial

	Yes	No
1. Do you have the cash in the bank to pay for the renovation?	_____	_____
2. Is that money free to use? (Not set aside for retirement, living expenses, medical costs, emergencies, and so on)?	_____	_____
3. If you spend the money in the bank, can you replace it within a year?	_____	_____
4. Within three years?	_____	_____
5. Would you feel comfortable increasing your overall monthly payments?	_____	_____
6. Do you know how much you can increase those payments before you feel uncomfortable?	_____	_____
7. Can you continue to maintain your existing lifestyle with increased monthly payments?	_____	_____
8. Can you sustain those increased monthly payments for at least three years?	_____	_____
9. For five years?	_____	_____
10. Do you have a plan for borrowing and then paying back *all* the money you need for the renovation?	_____	_____

ANSWERS: You're allowed three "no" answers—to questions 1, 3, and 8. Otherwise, you'd better have answered "yes" to all. If you haven't, then you're probably not ready to borrow for renovation.

Figure 5-1 What Can You Afford?

counselor. Such an adviser can break down your income, expenses, and financial reserves and give you a very specific answer on afford-ability.

TRAP

Beware of "free" financial counselors who have their own agendas. They may be trying to sell you stock, insurance, real estate, or some other investment vehicle. You're better off paying for a financial analysis from a counselor with no ax to grind than getting a "free" analysis that's bent toward selling you a financial product.

Cash or Credit?

If you can afford to write out a check from your bank account for the renovation and never miss the money, then don't read any further. Just do it.

TIP

If you are considering paying for the project in cash, keep in mind the economic principle of "substitution." Cash spent on renovation has an added value that could come from using (substituting) it elsewhere. For example, spend it on renovating and you won't be able to collect interest on it. You won't be able to use it to buy stocks. You won't be able to use it to pay off other debt, and so on. Decide where the money will work best for you.

My own experience is that about half the people who renovate will need to borrow the funds. The percentage is even higher for younger renovators who are just getting started. They simply haven't had the time to accumulate much cash. (Many more mature renovators do have the cash.)

The Golden Rules of Borrowing

So, if you must borrow, what are your options? What is the best way to borrow the money? Here are five rules of borrowing that I've found to be helpful.

1. Always spend time looking for the lowest interest rate.
2. If you need low payments, go for the longest term.
3. If you can handle high payments, go for the shortest term.
4. Get a loan with tax-deductible interest.
5. Know your true conditions and costs of borrowing.

Always Spend Time Looking For the Lowest Interest Rate

This is not the no-brainer is seems to be. Sometimes it's hard to know which of several loans has the lowest rate. For example, you go to bank A and it offers you a three-year loan for 7 percent the first year and 9 percent for the remaining two years. Bank B offers 8 percent for full three years. Bank C offers 12 percent, but there's no interest charged for the first six months. Which bank has the lowest interest rate?

Before you get out your calculator, be aware that you can't really tell from the information given above. You need to know more. For example, is the loan amortized (paid off in equal installments) or interest-only? There's more interest on an interest-only loan because the balance you owe doesn't decline over time.

Lenders are very tricky when presenting information about their loans. They emphasize the positive of their product, while tending to overlook the negative points. Of course, many people rely on the APR (annual percentage rate) to tell them the true costs of borrowing. Don't. The APR is no longer a reliable measurement.

The reason is that today creative lenders have come up with all sorts of "garbage" fees that are not covered by the APR. As a result, a loan with a higher APR, but no garbage fees, may actually be cheaper in the long run than a loan with a low APR and lots of garbage fees.

Here's a simple way to compare loans. When borrowing money from any lender, ask how much the total interest and fees will be for the full length of the loan. For example, if you're borrowing $10,000 for three years, find out the total interest charged over that time, then add in all the fees for getting the loan. This is your true cost. Now go to the next lender and ask the same thing for the same amount for three years. When you're done, simply compare your total loan costs (the true amount you're being charged). Now you're comparing apples with apples and can figure out what your true costs are.

If You Need Low Payments, Go For the Longest Term

The longer you pay, the lower your payments. This is simple mathematics. If you borrow $10,000 amortized at 8 percent of your unpaid balance, your monthly payments will be $313 for three years, $203 for five years, $121 for 10 years. Of course, at the end of any of those time periods, you will owe zero.

On the other hand, you can pay interest only. In that case, your monthly payment will be only $67 a month! But you'll continue to owe the full $10,000.

Many people opt for low-payment interest-only home loans, figuring that price appreciation will cover the unpaid balance and it will all come out in the wash when they sell. Maybe so, but what they are actually doing is trading off a very low payment for reduced equity in their home.

If You Can Handle High Payments, Go For the Shortest Term

This is the corollary of the previous rule. The idea here is to pay off that renovation loan as quickly as possible. There are many reasons to do so:

- You can borrow the money again for another project.
- You reestablish your borrowing limits.
- You cut out the extra interest you're being charged for a longer term.

Keep in mind, however, there can be good reasons for keeping a loan and not paying it off. See the section on deductibility below.

Get a Loan with Tax-Deductible Interest

Years ago all interest was deductible. Not so today. Interest on credit cards, for example, is not deductible. Interest for personal loans is not deductible.

But interest on a real estate loan, up to certain limits, may be deductible. Generally speaking, when you purchase a home, the interest on the mortgage up to $1 million may be tax deductible. Further, if you refinance, the interest on the refinancing up to $100,000 may be deductible. Certain rules apply, so check with your accountant.

If you can swing it, it obviously makes far more sense to borrow on a loan where you can deduct your interest than on one you can't.

TRAP

Be sure, before you borrow, that you can deduct the interest. Don't relay on the lender's assertions. Some lenders will say almost anything to get you to borrow and others may simply not know in your situation. Check with a good accountant or CPA who is familiar with your tax situation.

Know Your True Conditions and Costs of Borrowing

Be aware of special loan conditions that may affect you. For example, today many home equity loans contain prepayment clauses. They will typically say that if you pay the loan off before three years, you will owe a substantial penalty, sometimes $500 or more.

Also, many home equity loans require that you personally occupy the property. If you rent it out, you may be violating the conditions of the loan, and the lender could call in the entire amount or refuse to lend you more (in the case of a line of revolving credit).

In the case of credit card loans, be aware that the interest rate the lender charges is not regulated (with a very few exceptions in certain states that still retain usury laws). A common practice today is to issue cards with a relatively low interest rate—say, 7 percent. Then the original lender sells your account to another lender that changes the conditions of the account and ups the rate to 20 percent or higher.

Also be aware of all the conditions of your loan: which ones are cast in stone, which ones can be changed, and which ones are most likely to affect you.

And, know your true costs. The true interest rate on the money you borrow, which we calculated above, may be different from your actual cost for borrowing funds.

For example, you may have $10,000 invested in the stock market earning you 11 percent. If you cash in your stocks to pay for a renovation, you lose that 11 percent you would otherwise get. On the other hand, you may be able to get a loan for a true interest rate of 8 percent. By keeping your stock and borrowing the money, you're actually making a 3 percent profit.

When Should I Borrow the Money?

Borrow the money only as you need it. But arrange for *all* the financing before you begin the project.

Under an ideal financing arrangement, you get the cash as the renovation work requires it. For example, the contractor wants $2500 up front, so you borrow that. Several weeks later the contractor wants another $2500, so then you borrow that amount. After a month, the project is done and the contractor wants the balance of $5000. Only then do you borrow that final amount.

However, before you borrow anything, in the above example, arrange for a total line of credit of $10,000. You've got the money ready, but you don't borrow it until you need it—thus you don't pay any unnecessary interest.

TIP

Plan ahead. Even if you can get funded in a couple of weeks, it may take you several months to comparison-shop for the lowest interest rate and best terms. It won't hurt to start looking for financing long before you actually are going to need the money.

Why Should I Arrange For All Financing Up Front?

One of the big problems that renovators face is coming up with additional money after the project has begun. This occurs because they do not borrow enough initially to cover the entire project.

What's the problem with borrowing more, later? Quite simply, you may not be able to get it. The easiest example is borrowing on a credit card. Here the only issue is your credit limit and available credit. Until you reach your limit, you'll be able to continue borrowing funds.

However, what happens if you need more than your credit limit? Many times (but not always) lenders will increase these limits for good customers. But they may not increase it sufficiently for your needs. Or they may hesitate to increase it again if you come back a week later wanting more. Thus, at the least, you want to be sure your credit limit is high enough to cover the entire project.

On the other hand, if you're getting a construction or home improvement loan, you may be precluded from borrowing more once the project starts.

TRAP

Don't get caught short. Borrow all you'll need up front.

Where Can I Borrow the Money?

You can borrow from a bank, a savings and loan, a credit union, or a mortgage banker. You can even borrow the money online over the Internet. Here are the most common types of borrowing.

FHA Title 1. These are mortgages insured by the federal government. The biggest advantage is their high loan-to-value ratio (how much of your home's value you can borrow against).

Pros   Financing up to the full value (100 percent) of your home

                   Competitive interest rates

                   Usually quick funding

Interest deductible up to limits

Minimal appraisal required

Available from most banks

Cons   Maximum loan limit (currently $25,000)

Money must be used for functional repairs or renovation (not for adding a spa)

Home must be owner-occupied

TIP

Become familiar with LTV (loan-to-value) ratios if you're going to put your property up as collateral. An LTV is the percentage of the home's appraised value the lender will loan. For example, an 80 percent LTV on a $100,000 house is $80,000—the maximum loan. All lenders on real estate live by LTV limits. Some will lend only 80 percent LTV. Some put the limit at 60 percent, while others go to 90 percent or higher. Also, be aware of CLTV (combined loan-to-value) ratios, which are based on the total of *all* the mortgage loans on your property. Similar limits may apply here as well.

Credit Cards.   A credit card loan is probably the most expensive way to borrow. You can simply get a cash advance to pay for labor costs, or charge the materials on your card.

Pros   Money readily available to anyone who has a credit card, up to its limits

No appraisal required

Available everywhere

Cons   Highest interest rates, often 18 to 24 percent

Interest not deductible

Home Improvement Loan.   A home improvement loan is actually a construction mortgage on your property. Your home is the collateral and you are paid as the work is done. Available from banks and some savings and loans, the loan is actually a second mortgage on your property. Thus you have two payments—your existing first mortgage and the new home improvement loan. Generally, you must maintain a loan-to-value ratio of 80 percent, but you are allowed to add construction costs to the value of your property.

Pros	Usually available for full amount of renovation
	Competitive interest rates
	Interest deductible up to limits
Cons	Lender holds back the money in stages until the work is completed, often causing significant delays
	Money can be used only for the renovation project, not for living expenses
	Home must qualify through appraisal
	Borrower must fill out lots of paperwork and come up with complete plans, estimates, and a list of contractors
	Home must be owner-occupied

Home Equity Loan.   A home equity loan is like a home improvement loan in that it puts a second mortgage on your property. However, use of the money is not restricted to just home improvement.

Pros	Can be used for any purpose
	Competitive interest rates
	Interest usually deductible up to limits
	Quick funding, usually within two weeks
	Usually available as a revolving line of credit, allowing you to borrow up to the maximum at any time and pay back any amount at any time
Cons	Usually limited to 80 percent loan-to-value ratio (loan cannot be more than 80 percent of your home's value)
	Often contains a substantial prepayment penalty if you want to sell or refinance and have the home equity loan removed
	Home must qualify through appraisal
	Home must be owner-occupied

TRAP

Beware of new mortgages offered for more than your home's value—typically advertised as 125 percent mortgages. The interest rate is often higher than the going market rate. Further, the IRS may consider all or a portion of the amount to be a personal loan. Thus, the interest may not be tax-deductible, and the loan may tie up both the property and you personally.

Unsecured Line of Credit.   More and more banks are offering unsecured lines of credit to their better customers. Unsecured means that you need not put up any collateral for the loan.

Pros	Once established, money available on demand.
	Revolving line (borrow and repay up to maximum as often as you like)
	Can be used for any purpose
	No appraisal of property required
Cons	Higher interest rate than for mortgages
	Interest not deductible
	Hard to get for many borrowers

Refinancing.   Here you get a new and larger first mortgage. The new mortgage gives you enough money to pay off the old one (done automatically when you borrow) with cash left over to pay for the renovation work you want to do.

TIP

Many varieties of refinancing are available, but they usually come down to two basic types: adjustable-rate mortgages (ARMs), in which the interest rate adjusts up or down depending on market conditions, and fixed-rate mortgages, in which the interest rate does not change over the life of the loan. The rule is, get fixed-rate refinancing when market rates are low to lock in the low interest. Get an ARM when market rates are very high, so your interest rate will drop as the market eventually goes down.

Pros Lowest possible interest rate for a mortgage

    Longest terms (up to 30 years)

    Great variety (adjustable or fixed rates)

    Interest is deductible up to limits

Cons Strict qualifications for borrowers

    Loan-to-value ratio usually limited to 80 or 90 percent

    Home usually must be owner-occupied

TRAP

Be sure you know what the true interest rate on an ARM is. Most will offer a low "teaser" rate to hook you and then, after a few months, raise your rate sky high.

Life Insurance Loans. Here you borrow money on the cash value of a life insurance policy.

Pros Very low interest rate

    Attractive payback periods

    Limited to a percentage of the cash value of your life insurance

Cons Interest not deductible

    Lowers the value of your life insurance

Rehab Credits. Many utility companies will give you a credit or even a cash payment if you do certain work such as installing extra insulation, adding weather stripping around doors and windows, or installing a more efficient water heater or furnace. Contact your local utility company for more information on any rehab programs available.

Pros The money is usually paid directly to you in cash

    It is not a loan, so you don't need to pay it back

Cons Often only for a small percentage (10 to 35 percent) of the cost of the work

Must provide proof of purchase and work done

Limited to certain projects

Borrowing from Relatives or Friends

Many people have rich relatives and, if the relationship is good, borrow from them. If it works for you, fine. However, my own feeling is that you run too great a risk of ruining a relationship over money. My rule is, never borrow from a relative or friend unless you absolutely must (and renovations are not in that category).

If you decide to borrow from a relative or friend, however, you can help limit the risk of ruining the relationship by being businesslike. By that I mean, draw up a loan agreement in which you spell out:

- The full amount borrowed and when and how it will be paid back.

- The amount of interest you will pay.

- What, if anything, you're putting up as collateral. If it's a second mortgage on your property, have the arrangement done properly through a title insurance company and record it.

- All other terms of the loan.

TRAP

The IRS feels that almost any loan should bear interest. If a friend or relative refuses to charge interest, be aware that the IRS could calculate interest equal to the going rate for the loan and then tax that interest.

6

All about Plans and Permissions

Do you really need a set of plans for your renovation project?

That depends on what you want to do. If you're simply changing an old faucet in the bathroom for a new designer model, then you hardly need plans. (If you do it yourself, of course, you'll need to follow the instruction sheet that comes with the new faucet assembly.)

On the other hand, if you're renovating the whole house, a kitchen, or a bathroom, or even if you're just changing the decor of your home, a set of plans is helpful, if not crucial. The plans are your road map to where you want to go. They clearly show your journey from before to after. Without a good set of plans, you could end up in foreign territory with a job that looks amateurish and may need to be redone.

Of course, the plans don't always need to be formal. Sometimes just sketches of the final layout are all that are needed. This is particularly the case with interior redesigns. Other times, you'll need actual blueprints for contractors to follow.

Can I Draw the Plans Myself?

There is no one to say you can't draw the plans yourself, although you may not want to. We'll discuss getting others to draw the plans for you shortly.

A friend of mine took a drafting course in high school, and that was enough to allow her to draw plans that she's used successfully for whole-house renovations—indeed, for building homes from the ground up. The simpler the project, the easier it is to do the plans.

For example, there's no reason you can't sketch out where you want a new greenhouse window to go or where some new cabinets will be placed.

On the other hand, the more complex the plans, the greater your knowledge will need to be. If you're adding a room, you'll want to show foundation, roof, rafters, studs, ceiling, electrical, and possibly even plumbing. If you don't know the conventions for showing these features, you will undoubtedly want to get help and probably have a pro do the plans for you.

TIP

Remember, the only things that plans are for is to show what you want done. As long as you can get that across clearly, you've done the job.

TRAP

Renovation means not only adding new, but tearing out old. When you break into a wall, you never know what you will find. There might be a diagonal brace right where you want to place a window, or electrical wiring or plumbing where you want to put a door. The plans, therefore, are only guides. Your really creative work will come once you see what your true obstacles are.

A quick word about home-drawn plans and building department approval. I've never known a building department to refuse approval of home-drawn plans, regardless of the size of the project, if they were drawn correctly and clearly. Nobody says you must use a professional.

What about Engineering?

If you get into a renovation project that involves the actual structure of the home—such as moving walls, ceilings, or floors—your plans will need to be engineered. That's usually more complicated than it sounds.

What's typically involved is being sure you are using heavy enough wood (assuming you're not using steel) to handle the various weight loads in your home. For example, a floor may require a minimum of 40 pounds per square foot. Your supports from foundation to joists must be able to handle this load.

Also, you must have enough studs of the right size and quality in the walls (usually 2 × 4s or 2 × 6s at 16 inches on center). With doors and windows you must have the right-size headers (heavy wood beams whose size is determined by the width of the opening), and the doors and windows themselves must be between minimum and maximum height and width. You can get this information and more from books on construction techniques, readily available in bookstores. Try *Renovation: A Complete Guide,* by Michael W. Litchfield (Sterling Publishers, 1997), for starters.

However, your project may involve a very wide opening, use of steel supports, snowloads on the roof, or special considerations in the foundation. When that happens, you will need to get the plans professionally engineered. An engineer will look them over and tell you the precise type and size of materials to use. For this, you'll need to consult a local firm that handles structural engineering (check your phone book).

I've taken my plans to structural engineering firms and for a few hundred dollars had them do the engineering and write the measurements right on the plans. When the engineering firm adds a signature and title, it's your go-ahead for the building department.

There are other types of engineering problems. For example, you might be building on a hillside, or the soil might be wet or expansive. You could need a soils engineering report that specifies a thicker or deeper foundation, or a specific electrical problem that requires an electrical engineer's report.

The list is endless. The good news is that 85 percent of the time, as noted earlier, you need only minor engineering work that you can do yourself.

Should I Get Professionally Drawn Plans?

The easiest, though definitely not the cheapest, way to get a good set of plans is to have them professionally drawn. An architect should be able to come up with a decent set of plans for you. However, be prepared to handle the tab. Architects charge a percentage of the overall building costs for the plans, with a minimum fee.

On major remodeling projects, an architect can help not only with the plans but also with the design and with suggestions about what to do. Keep in mind that architects are trained to work backward—that is, to envision the finished product, then work back toward a set of plans that will achieve it. Thus working with an architect, especially one who specializes in remodeling, can be a very good way to come up with a great-looking final product.

If you want to save money and have your own vision of what you want done, consider using the services of a draftsperson. This is someone who specializes in drawing building plans (and often works for an architect). If you have detailed drawings of what you want, along with a floor plan of how things should be laid out, a draftsperson can often come up with a set of plans for a fraction of the cost of an architect. But don't expect the advice and direction that only an architect can give.

Check the phone book for both architects and draftspeople (look under drafting services). You can also ask contractors or materials sellers for a recommendation.

What Kinds of Plan Approvals Do I Need?

Approval depends on where you live and the type of work you're planning to do. Some jobs require no approval of any kind. Others require at least three approvals.

You *don't* need a permit if you're going to move the cabinets around your kitchen (without affecting the sink or stove), if you're going to install a new tile floor in the entryway, or if you're going to be painting and wallpapering throughout the house.

As long as all the work is done inside the home; as long as it doesn't involve plumbing, electrical, heating, air-conditioning, and other home systems; as long as there are no structural, health, or safety issues, you don't need a permit and you don't usually need the approval of anyone. Just get started and do it.

TRAP

There are exceptions where you do need approval for all-in-the-home work. One is when you're living in a condo, co-op, or townhouse. Any type of construction will involve dust, dirt, noise, and so on. There may be restrictions in your bylaws prohibiting work done between certain hours. You may need to get approval of your homeowners association to do almost any kind of renovation. Check first.

Homeowner Approval

If you own a condo, townhouse, or co-op, the first approval you will likely need, and sometimes the hardest to get, is from your home-owners association (or your board of directors).

Typically, you will need to prepare a detailed set of plans (at least good enough for an average person to clearly see what you intend to do) and submit it to the organization. Undoubtedly there will be an architectural committee to review your plans, making sure that whatever changes you propose are within the parameters of what the condo or co-op allows.

For example, you may want to change a conventional window to a greenhouse window that extends a foot beyond your home. However, your homeowners association may turn down your request, stating that the bylaws do not allow any windows to protrude beyond the surface of the exterior walls of the building. You've just been shot down.

TRAP

Many single-family homes built in tracts also have homeowners associations, primarily to enforce strict architectural standards. You will know if you have one because it will send you a bill monthly or annually, and/or an official of the board may stop by occasionally to talk with you about homeowner matters. Also, you should have been given information about a homeowners association at the time you purchased your home.

Of course, you can ask the architectural committee to reconsider or you may appeal the decision to the full board. But if the organization is intent on maintaining rules of conformity (which it usually is), you may not be able to go forward with your project, or may have to change it to conform to the bylaws. For more information on dealing with homeowners boards, check into my book *Tips and Traps When Purchasing a Condo, Townhouse, or Co-op,* (McGraw-Hill, 1999).

If you need and don't get homeowner approval, yet still proceed with the project, the homeowners association may fine you and put a lien against your property. It may even go to court to halt work. In short, it's not something to take lightly or ignore.

Once you get homeowners approval, if it is needed, your next step is usually the local planning department.

Planning Department Approval

The planning department, in the absence of a homeowners association, usually enforces the CC&Rs (conditions, covenants, and restrictions) that run with the title to your property as well as the local planning code.

The CC&Rs are much like the bylaws of a homeowners association, except they are not usually as strict. They do, however, restrict what can be done with your home. For example, they may specify the minimum amount of square feet that can be built on any floor. You want to add a second floor of 400 square feet, but the CC&Rs specify that the minimum for a second floor is 800 square feet. Either you add more or you abandon the project.

The CC&Rs can be even more specific, detailing the colors you can paint the exterior, the type of roof (tile, wood, or composition shingle) you can use, or even the type of landscaping you may have.

The local planning code is often part of a master plan for your area. It specifies such things as the "setback"—how far from the street and other houses your house may be—and even the maximum height of a building. You can easily get into trouble here when you make additions. Suppose there is a 10-foot minimum sideyard setback requirement and you have only 10 feet between your house and your neighbor's. You want to add 5 feet onto the side of your home, reducing the sideyard setback to half the minimum required. Your plan would be rejected.

If your work doesn't involve changing the footprint of the home, chances of getting planning department approval are much greater.

It will be more difficult, as noted, with exterior changes. Once you do get approval, however, your next step is the building department.

TIP

You can always appeal the planning department's decision and try to get a variance. This is a special exemption just for you. Normally you won't get a variance approval unless you can demonstrate that your changes won't be detrimental to neighbors or won't substantially alter the overall general plan. To be successful, you often have to get all the affected neighbors to sign a statement in favor of what you want to do, plus provide the planning department with compelling reasons why you should be allowed to move forward. You will also have to pay a fee. Sometimes, in order to get a variance, you will want to go over the head of the planning department and take the entire matter to the local council. Obviously, much time and effort are involved. And I would put your chances of success at less than 50/50, depending on the circumstances involved.

Building Department Approval

The building department enforces the local building code. Often the local code is actually the UBC (Uniform Building Code) with additions for your area to make it stricter in certain ways. (For example, your area may have expansive soil and the local building department may insist on deeper footings.) The UBC is a comprehensive code for building construction throughout the United States.

TIP

I like to use the word "minimum" with regard to a building code, because in some cases the code may not be as strict as you would like. For example, it may specify a 100-pound snowload in your area, but you want to build forever and go for a 150-pound snowload. Or it may not require a catchpan under a propane heating system, but for additional safety, you install one anyway. (Propane is heavier than air and leaks tend to gather gas at a low level—a pan catches the leaking gas and vents it to the outside.) Sometimes you'll want to exceed the code.

You will need to get a building permit for work involving any major change to your home:

- Structural changes of any kind
- Plumbing—all but the smallest jobs, such as changing a washer
- Electrical changes involving rewiring or installing fixtures in new locations
- Gas—any changes at all
- Heating/air conditioning or any built-in system
- Insulation
- Spa or pool—adding or changing

TRAP

Don't think that just because you're replacing something that already exists, you don't need a permit. For example, most areas require a permit when replacing a dishwasher, even though you're simply connecting a new appliance to the old wiring and plumbing. The reason is to be sure that you connect a proper air gap—a safety feature. The same holds true with water heaters (to be sure the gas is properly connected and a pressure/temperature safety valve is installed) and many other common household items.

What's the Procedure for Getting a Permit?

The procedure for getting a permit is relatively simple. You appear at the building department, with your set of plans stamped with approvals from the homeowners association (if any) and the planning department, and simply say you want a permit.

The clerk will ask what you plan to do to determine what kind of permits you need. After that's done, you'll be hit with a fee (described below) and then told how long it will be before approval is given. Sometimes it's just a few days, but if the building department is large and busy, it could be a month or more. During that time your plans will be checked to be sure they are in compliance with the local building code.

After the compliance check, you'll be notified that your plans are ready. Once you pick them up, stamped with a building department approval, you can begin construction. However, you'll need to have the plans on hand at the site at all times, for review by a building inspector.

What If There's a Problem with the Plan Check?

Unless your plans were professionally drawn up (and even then), don't be surprised if you receive word that they require modification. I'm convinced that the plan checkers don't really feel they are doing their job unless they can find at least one item needing modification in every set of plans.

If you're lucky, the problem will be minor, often a discrepancy over engineering. You need to use a bigger header over a door or move the outlet in the bathroom farther away from the tub. (Electrical outlets generally can't be closer than 5 feet to a tub or shower.)

So you take the plans home, have the modifications made, and resubmit. Usually the second plan check is swift and you'll quickly get your okay to begin.

On the other hand, sometimes your whole concept may be rejected. You may want to add a wood- or gas-burning stove in your master bedroom, but the building department frowns on such stoves in bedroom areas, since they could cause suffocation to those sleeping there (by using up all the oxygen in the room). Yes, the department will let you use a gas or wood stove, *but* (1) the stove must have a direct outlet for fumes plus an exterior inlet for air and (2) the combustion area must be sealed so no room air is used.

Now, either you change the heater you're planning to get to meet the requirements (usually meaning you'll have to buy a more expensive one) or you don't put a stove in the master bedroom.

Sometimes the building department will simply nix the whole idea. For example, you may be in a rural area where septic tanks are used. You have three bedrooms in your house and you want to add a fourth. But the building department says that four bedrooms require three bathrooms, not two. So you need to add another bathroom. Okay, you think, I'll do it. The house needs another bathroom anyway.

Not quite, the building department says. In order to add another bathroom, you need to enlarge your septic tank. And you can't get a permit for a bigger tank because you don't have enough room on your property for a larger leach field. (The leach field in a septic system allows liquid waste to drain back into the soil.) The building department has, in effect, quashed the project.

What the Building Department Doesn't Know...

Sometimes the cost of a building permit (described below), the hassle involved, and the changes required make renovators dream about forgetting the permit. Why not just go ahead and not tell the building department? This is particularly tempting if all the work is inside: Who's to know the difference?

There are a number of serious problems here. First, the building code is basically a "health and safety" code. It's designed to ensure that whatever construction work is done will leave the property in a safe, habitable condition. If your planned work doesn't meet code, it simply may not be safe. And if it does meet code, why not get the permit?

Second, if you do the work without a permit, you may run into trouble when you resell. A good home inspection will almost certainly reveal work done without a permit. (As part of a good home inspection, the inspector, the real estate agent, or you should get a list from the building department of all permits on file.)

Most work that differs from what's standard for your home will stand out. If there's no permit, the buyers will undoubtedly demand that the work be brought up to code (a permit obtained) before they make a purchase. That could mean redoing the entire job, a very costly procedure!

A case in point: Peter did renovations as a sort of hobby (buying homes to live in, fixing them up, and then reselling). But he refused to take out permits, complaining about the cost and the trouble of hassling with a building inspector. He would say, "If there's a question when I resell, I'll get the permit then."

Peter did good work and for a long time there were no problems. Then, one day, a buyer questioned a room addition. Peter admitted he didn't have a permit. The buyer demanded that the room be brought up to code as evidenced by a permit.

So Peter applied for a permit. By this time, of course, the room was finished—wallboard in place, electrical outlets installed, walls painted and ready. The building inspector demanded that Peter rip everything out. He wanted to see the size of the studs used, their placement, the type and gauge of electrical wire used, whether wires were anchored near every outlet box, whether there was appropriate insulation in the exterior walls, and on and on. In other words, before a final inspection, there had to be many rough inspections to check the work. Of course, Peter couldn't do these because he had already finished the job.

So, in order to get the permit, Peter had to rip the job down to the bare wood and, for practical purposes, start over. At first he balked, saying he would find another, less demanding buyer. But he already had applied for the permit and the city would hound him until either the work was properly completed or it was totally ripped out. Further, because of disclosure laws, which apply to most real estate sales today, Peter would be required to disclose the problems with the room to any new buyer. He simply gritted his teeth, did the work, and paid the bills.

All of which is to say: It's often cheaper to get a permit than try to avoid it.

TRAP

 As soon as you get a permit, information about the job is forwarded to the assessor's office. When you complete the work, a notice of completion is likewise forwarded and you can expect the tax assessor to raise your taxes according to the amount and cost of work done. Some people don't want to get permits to avoid having to pay additional taxes. Their desire is understandable. Realistically, however, a permit and the accompanying reassessment are unavoidable. You just have to grit your teeth and bear it.

What Do Building Permits Cost?

There are fees for building permits. Cities and counties often use their own fee structure, based on their estimate of the cost of the work done or the type of work. The smallest jobs may require a fee of $35 to $100. For larger jobs the permit fees may run into the hundreds or sometimes thousands of dollars. You can typically expect to pay 2 to 3 percent of the total cost of the work for permits.

The permit fees usually include the following:

- Plan check
- Inspections
- Paperwork

Keep in mind that you may need several permits. On a major kitchen remodeling project, for example, you would likely need:

- Construction permit for structural changes
- Electrical permit for lighting, appliances, and other electrical work
- Gas and plumbing permit (usually one) for sinks, dishwasher, gas stove, and so on

There could be other permit requirements, depending on the work done. In addition, there may be other fees. For example, you may need to make a refundable deposit, to ensure against damage to the street or sidewalk, if the building department thinks you may move in heavy machinery. There may be a fee for additional flow to the sewer system if you're adding a bathroom.

The building permit fees can be substantial, and you should try to figure them in when you make your final estimates of cost.

Who Gets the Approvals and Permits?

It takes time to get approvals and permits. You may have to appear before a board of directors for your homeowners or co-op association. You may need to spend several hours at the planning and/or building department.

If you have your contractor get the approvals and permits, expect to be hit with a charge for the time spent. After all, it's work away from the job site for the contractor.

If it's a big job, such as a room addition or a bathroom or kitchen makeover, the contractor will probably figure in the cost of getting approval and just take care of it.

On the other hand, if it's a small job, the contractor may ask for an hourly rate to get the permits or simply suggest that you take care of them. If you go down and get the permits yourself, you'll save some money.

TIP

The building department will ask for the name of your contractor. If you're doing the work yourself, the building department may balk, saying that it would prefer a contractor do the work. However, there is no law to prevent you from doing the work yourself. In this case the building department may require you to sign a statement indicating that you reside at the property and will continue to live there yourself for six months to a year after the work is done. Such a statement is particularly important if you're doing work involving gas, electricity, or plumbing. The residency requirement simply makes the assumption that you will do a good and safe job if you're going to inhabit the property.

Do I Need a Survey?

A survey is a check of the boundary lines of your property. It can be essential in the purchase of a property, particularly in rural areas, where property lines are not easy discerned. It is less necessary in urban areas, where property lines are often well defined.

When renovating, if you are adding a room or even a fireplace that enlarges the outside perimeter of your home, a survey may be beneficial or even a necessity. For example, if you are adding to the side or the back of your home, you may be encroaching into the setback areas required between houses. However, you can't tell if you're encroaching unless you know the exact property line.

In a tract home, the property line is often presumed to be the fence that divides neighbors. But you may have no fence and there may not be an obvious division between properties. Therefore, to find out the exact boundary, you will need to call in a surveyor.

TRAP

Be careful of assuming where a property line is. Just because a fence is between neighbors doesn't mean it's on the property line. The fence could be a foot or more on one property or the other, as is sometimes the case when the fence follows the lay of the land rather than the property line. To be safe, always call in a surveyor.

To simply determine a single property line, a surveyor may have a minimum fee, anywhere between $100 and $250. This is just to pay for the cost of coming out, locating the survey marks in your area, and then indicating them (usually with red flags on short picks driven into the earth or hung on a fence or tree). It costs much more for a full property survey, which derives all boundaries and, perhaps, even easements.

From the boundary line, you can then accurately measure the setback (which you can find by a visit to your local planning/building department) using a tape measure.

Getting plans and permissions is a normal part of most renovation projects. If you don't fight it, but just understand that approval is part of the job, the process should go quickly and easily.

7

Hiring the Right Contractor

Getting the right person to do your renovation is critical, since it will determine the cost and the quality of the result. Hire well, and you'll come out very pleased. Hire badly, and you'll regret it every time you look at the work.

Should I Hire Myself as Contractor?

The first issue, really, is whether you need a contractor (preferably one who specializes in renovations) or whether you can do the work yourself. To answer that, you need to know what's involved. There are two types of contractors on a job: the general contractor and the subcontractor.

The general contractor is the overall coordinator of the job. He or she follows the work through from start to finish and oversees the big jobs as well as the tiniest details. This is the person who sees to it that *all* the work is done.

Duties of a General Contractor
- Supervise all phases of work and see that plans are carried out.
- Hire, supervise, and pay subcontractors.
- Buy some materials necessary to finish the job.
- Coordinate all initial demolition and later cleanup.
- Deal with building department inspectors.
- Get approvals from the building department.
- Work with and get approval from homeowner.

TRAP

In most renovations, you'll continue to live in the house while the work is being done. That means you'll be in close contact with the contractor. In such a case, be absolutely sure you feel comfortable and trust the people in your home.

For doing all the above, the general contractor charges a fee, typically from 15 to 35 percent or more of the overall cost, depending on how much work the general contractor actually does. The issue becomes: Can you do the work of the general contractor yourself? What are the pros and cons?

TIP

A general contractor is licensed to handle the overall work and, in the case of renovations, is sometimes called a remodeling contractor. A subcontractor is a licensed specialist—such as a carpenter, plumber, or electrician—who "subs" work from a general contractor. It's important to understand that subs are almost always more than willing to work directly for you.

Doing It Yourself Versus Hiring It Out

Money Versus Sweat

If you hire a general contractor, it will cost you more. On the other hand, if you hire a general contractor, you can simply be a bystander and drop by occasionally to watch the work progress. You don't need to get your hands dirty. Best of all, when something goes wrong, you can rant and rave at someone else! In short, you pay for having the contractor do all the work and take all the blame.

The Fun of Doing It Yourself

For most people, it's a lot of fun doing a renovation, big or small. You can get in there and participate. You can make materials, labor, and money decisions. You can see something take shape that you yourself create. Perhaps best of all, you get bragging rights when it's finished!

The big question is: Are you competent to do the work of a general contractor? Can you hire subcontractors, follow plans, buy materials, and so on? (Do you have the time to do this?) Only you can say. My own feeling is that if you think you can do the work of a general contractor for your own job, you probably can.

TIP

Usually people who have had previous experience in building projects and in general are "handy" have the confidence to begin. And they usually succeed.

TRAP

Beware of biting off more than you can chew. You may think you can do the work of a general contractor simply because you are totally unaware of what's involved. If you haven't previously worked with subcontractors, haven't done renovation work yourself, or are undertaking an unusually big project, you should seriously consider the services of a general contractor—at least this first time out.

What Do I Have to Do When I'm My Own Contractor?

In addition to taking care of all the details, such as cleanup and perhaps demolition, you'll need to do the following:

- Find subcontractors.
- Negotiate contracts with them.
- Handle the purchase of materials.
- Direct and supervise their work.
- Be on call to accept materials deliveries.

- Inspect the job on regular occasions.
- Pay for materials and work.
- Deal with building inspectors.
- Do all the work that a general contractor would otherwise do.

TIP

If you decide to be your own contractor, consider hiring a lieutenant. You may be able to pay one of the workers who is frequently on the job site, or who lives nearby, to handle some of the supervisory work for you.

Where Do I Find a Good Contractor?

If you decide to hire a contractor, there are the usual places to look, such as the Yellow Pages, Web sites (where many contractors advertise today), and building contractors' directories in local newspapers and magazines. Many contractors advertise in newspapers as well.

Better sources are personal recommendations of friends, relatives, and associates who have had work done by contractors. Typically these people will either rave over the wonderful job done or rant at the terrible experience they had. It can tell you a lot.

In addition, ask for *personal* recommendations from local real estate agents and building materials suppliers. Find out if the person has worked specifically with the contractor in the past.

TRAP

Contractors make their living not only from their work but also from their ability to get work. In other words, they soon learn to be very nice to customers, or they wash out. Thus, don't be blinded by the fact that the contractor seems to be "such a nice guy/gal." Expect contractors to be very nice, but be on your guard too.

You can also contact the National Association of the Remodeling Industry at (703) 276-7600 or www.nari.com, and the local offices of building and trade associations. Finally, if you see renovation work being done in your neighborhood, stop by and ask if you can take a closer look. Talk to the contractor involved. It's a good way to get leads.

TIP

Once you've found a contractor you like, ask for recommendations of other suppliers. Contractors almost always can suggest people in every line of construction work. You can thus network your way to really good people.

What Should I Look For in a Contractor?

When you meet a contractor, chances are he or she will want to look at your plans, if you have any, as well as the site itself. The contractor will ask you all sorts of questions. For each one the contractor asks, ask and get an answer to your own question. You should ask the contractor at least the following questions.

Question 1: "Have You Done This Type of Work Before and Can You Supply References?"

Once you've located a contractor, be sure to find out what jobs he or she is currently working on and if you can go over and check them out. Look to see if the past work is similar to the sort of work you want done.

Ask for references. Contractors often carry a photo album showing examples of their work. Ask for the name and number of the people who had the work done. Then call.

Find out if the homeowners liked the finished work, if there were any difficulties along the way, and if they can give a good recommendation. If the project done is similar to yours, you may even get invited out to see the contractor's work firsthand.

My own rule is never to hire a contractor unless I first get a recommendation and can see the work that was done. This is a vital
step and you should not overlook it. It's far too late when you're
into the job to learn that the contractor is sloppy or does only
mediocre work.

Question 2: "Will You Yourself Do the Actual Work?"

The contractor may be nicest, sweetest person in the world with all
kinds of experience. But what good does that do you if the contractor then hires your job out to someone else who is less experienced
or careful?

TIP

If you're going to be working directly with the contractor, find out if your personalities mix. Talk to the person for a while. Does he or she have a family? How does
the contractor feel about working with others? You
don't want to learn too late that the person you've
hired does things only one way: his or her way.

You want the person you hire to be the one who actually does the
work. Don't accept substitutes. You could get a bum job.

Question 3: "Are You Licensed?"

All states license contractors. However, not everyone who wants to
work for you will have a license. Should you insist on hiring only
licensed people?
The safe answer is yes. There are good reasons.

- You can call the state licensing board to find out if there are complaints against the contractor or if his or her license has been
  revoked or suspended.

- If a licensed contractor messes up the job, you can sue to recover
  damages more easily in small claims court. (The presumption is
  that a licensed contractor knows what he or she is doing.)

- If you have a disagreement with the contractor, you can threaten to file a complaint with the state licensing board. That will sometimes get the contractor to see things your way.

TRAP

Just because the state licenses the contractor, doesn't mean it does a good job of policing. In many states the licensing board takes action only in the most severe circumstances and only after repeated complaints. Further, in many states the complaints against contractors are not made easily available to the public. Just because a contractor has a license is not a guarantee of good service.

On the other hand, you may find someone without a license who is willing to do the job for less. And that person may provide many references from homeowners who were all extremely pleased with the work.

Still be wary, however. The unlicensed contractor typically does not have insurance, which could be a problem for you if there's an injury on the job. Further, the unlicensed contractor may have difficulty in getting good prices for materials, which could end up costing you more for the job in the long run.

I've worked both ways. Generally, I won't hire unlicensed contractors to do any major work. For the small jobs, however, I will consider them.

Question 4: "Do You Have Workers' Compensation?"

People get injured on the job all the time. Renovation, just like new construction, carries with it some degree of hazard. Therefore, you want to be sure that the contractor carries insurance to cover injuries. This is usually in the form of state workers' compensation.

When you are your own contractor, it is usually up to you to see to it that the people you employ are covered. Indeed, in some states it may even be considered illegal to employ a person without providing workers' compensation.

TIP

Be sure to ask to see a current workers' comp policy. Also, check with your homeowner policy. It may offer you workers' comp automatically, at least for small jobs that you've contracted.

Be aware that in today's workplace, many people do not have health insurance. That means if they get injured on the job and there is no workers' compensation to cover the injury, their only recourse may be to sue you.

Question 5: "Can You Post a Performance Bond?"

Posting a bond is usually of concern when you hire a general contractor and when the job is for a substantial amount of money. A performance bond essentially promises that if the contractor can't finish the job in a workmanlike fashion, the bonding company will step in and see to it that the job is completed, up to the amount of money of the bond. Be aware that getting a bond involves a great deal of hassle, time, and paperwork.

TRAP

If you go with a contractor who doesn't post a bond, be sure you keep tight control of the money flow. For example, you may want to pay for materials yourself, and pay for work only as it's completed. (In the next chapter, we'll see how you can set up an account that lets the contractor order while you pay.) No, all this can't guarantee that you won't have problems, such as mechanic's liens (see Chapter 8), but it can help.

TIP

It takes very good credit, a lot of capital, and sterling past performance to be able to post a bond, plus it can cost up to 5 percent of the price of the contract.

However, to some extent, it's more important to know *if* a contractor can qualify for a bond than it is to actually get one.

Many, if not most, contractors will be unable or unwilling to post a performance bond. Does that mean you should eliminate those who can't or won't?

Not in my book. Generally speaking, contractors who are able to post a bond will have the very best records. But they may also be among the highest bidders. Yes, you can be fairly sure you're getting a Cadillac job with them. But perhaps you don't need that kind of assurance.

In the many projects that I've done, I've rarely had contractors post a bond. I've simply asked the contractors if they could, and been pleased to learn that, yes, it was something they could do. But I've rarely wanted to go through the expense and hassle of it myself.

If the recommendations were excellent, if the previous work, which I looked at, was to my liking, and if the person seemed decent and honest, I went with the contractor, regardless.

Question 6: "Can You Give Me a Total-Price Bid?"

It's important to remember that you're not building a rocket ship. You're simply doing a home renovation project. Further, the contractor has presumably done the sort of job you propose many times before. Therefore, there's no reason that a contractor can't give you a firm bid. By the way, a firm bid means, "I'll do all the work for $1500." Or $10,000, or whatever.

TRAP

The exception to a firm bid is when an unexpected problem crops up (usually during demolition) that requires a change in plans. However, most contractors will protect themselves by adding a clause to the contract for dealing with such unexpected occurrences. The clause allows them to add a certain amount to the price, usually on a time-plus-materials basis.

Some contractors, however, will prefer to give you a bid entirely for "time and materials." In other words, they will take the job at so much an hour plus the cost of materials. With such an open-ended contract, you really have no idea how much it will eventually cost you. This is the way the government pays companies to build rocket ships. Since it's never been done before—it's new and untested—the company will do the work only for time and materials. And, of course, you've heard of how these sorts of deals always save the government money, right?

TIP

A contractor who insists on a time-plus-materials contract is usually one who is inexperienced given the work you want done.

Sorry, I can't help being a bit sarcastic here. On occasion I have agreed to a time-plus-materials contract and have almost always regretted it. Inevitably it costs more, sometimes far more, than I thought the job should cost.

Remember, when you're paying for time and materials, there's no incentive on the part of the contractor to finish quickly or to use materials sparingly. Indeed, the incentives are in the other direction.

All of which is to say that I strongly recommend you get a contractor who will give you a firm full-price bid.

Question 7: "Can You Give Me Start and Finish Dates?"

The start date is when the actual work will begin. Often it just means the date that the materials will arrive, but at least you'll know that the project is beginning.

A finish date is the last date by which you can expect the project to be completed. For example, by March 15 all work will be done and signed off by the building department (if appropriate).

Contractors are loath to give start and particularly finish dates. The reason is that, especially when it comes to remodeling work, they make their living by doing several jobs simultaneously. They'll work a bit on yours, then a bit on mine, then on someone else's.

There's nothing wrong with this. Most construction work is done piecemeal. For example, a wall is framed. Then an electrician has to come and put in the wiring and electrical boxes. Then, if needed, a plumber has to run pipe. Then insulation has to be added (if it's an outside wall), followed by sheetrock, and on and on. Rarely is it possible for any one contractor to simply begin and continue on to the finish.

Thus, contractors will work a bit on one job until they get stopped, then move on to another. Their own best efficiency comes when they have several jobs to do simultaneously.

The problem is that with contracting, it's either feast or famine. There's either too much work or not enough. Thus, worrying about those famine times, contractors very frequently take on more work than they can comfortably handle; they want to be sure they have enough.

The results are those legendary delays. The contractor promises to be there on Monday, but doesn't arrive until Wednesday. Then the contractor works only half a day, leaves, and doesn't come back until the following week. All you see is your job, and you can't understand why the contractor doesn't just come in and finish it. The contractor, on the other hand, may be looking at two, three, perhaps half a dozen jobs, trying to do them all at once and keep everyone satisfied.

What you need to keep yourself from having a fit, and to be sure that the work gets done in a timely fashion, is a written start and finish date.

A few years ago a house I owned lost much of its roof during a hard winter. Snowfall was three times the normal annual rate, and the roof had to be shoveled off several times to prevent it from collapsing from the weight of accumulated snow.

When spring came, a great many shingles were torn off or broken. In short, the home needed a new roof. The problem, however, was that I wasn't alone. Many houses in the area also needed a new roof, and there was a shortage of roofers.

By the middle of summer and facing another winter without a secure roof, I was getting desperate. About that time an out-of-the-area roofer arrived and said he'd do the job. He was a licensed contractor, but all his references were 500 miles away and I couldn't check them out. He wanted 50 percent of the cost on signing and the rest on completion. (I'll have much more to say about contracts and how much and when you should pay in Chapter 8.)

As I say, I was desperate, so I signed on August 1 and the contractor said he'd get to it within a few weeks.

August rolled by and when September came, I called to see when he would start. I learned that he'd taken on a dozen or more other jobs in the area and simply couldn't get to mine. But he said he'd be there soon.

September ended and October rolled around, and along with it came the first suggestions of winter. Still no contractor. When I called, I learned that he was being sued by another person in the area for doing a lousy roofing job. Now I was really worried.

November and still no contractor. Finally, in mid-December, in the middle of a winter storm with snow falling lightly, he and his crew showed up and in a remarkable two days put up my roof.

In a way I was lucky the job got done even without firm start and end dates. But it was a great learning experience for me. From that point on, I never accepted a contract that didn't have a specific start and finish date, something I could haul the contractor to court on if he or she didn't perform.

Most contractors will go along with a specified start date, particularly if I'm willing to give them a few days or even weeks of flex time. On the other hand, few contractors like to have a finish date, since it could get them into trouble if they're doing too many jobs. Nevertheless, I also insist on it.

TIP

Be flexible on finish dates. Ask the contractor when he or she is likely to be finished, then tack a couple of weeks onto the finish date. If the contractor is still uncomfortable, add another week. You just want the work to be done in a timely fashion. If the contractor still refuses, you have to wonder why.

TRAP

Start and finish dates can work against you. If you add a few days to the beginning and a few weeks to the end, a savvy contractor could take all that time, when otherwise he or she might have finished in just a few days total!

Can I Save Money by Buying My Own Building Supplies?

Of course, you can buy almost any given item for less at a discount sale than your contractor will charge you for it. That's because the contractor builds in a markup on the item. So on the surface, it would appear that buying the materials yourself will save you money: on a big job, big money.

However, most contractors won't agree to work with you on that basis. They simply won't take the job *if* you insist on purchasing the materials yourself. Some renovators think the reason is that contractors want to pad their profits, make more money. Actually there's a much different motive.

When a contractor bids a job, he or she knows (presumably) what materials are required to finish the work and when they are needed. You, on the other hand, probably do not. Consider tile work.

You may be having someone retile a bathroom. You go to the hardware store and discover some tiles you would be happy with for $4 a square foot. On the other hand, the contractor shows you tiles, which you would swear are identical, and wants $6 a square foot.

You balk. Why should you pay the contractor 50 percent more for the tiles? So to save money, you try to make an arrangement whereby you'll supply the tiles and the contractor will supply only the work.

If you were a contractor, would you agree to such terms? Not if you wanted to survive in the business, and it has nothing to do with padding the markup.

What If Extra Materials Are Needed?

While you may indeed be able to buy the surface tiles for $4 a foot, what about the trim? (The trim often costs more than the surface tiles.) And exactly which trim pieces will you need? And how many of them? It's very unlikely you'll know.

TIP

Irwin's second law of renovation: You never know *exactly* how much or which materials you'll need until you're halfway through the job.

Even if the contractor specifies the trim pieces that he or she will need, it's almost always the case that needs change after the job starts. Extra or different pieces are suddenly required. Now, who goes to the store to get them? If it's the contractor, it's on his or her time, which is not being paid for because you're buying the materials. (That time going to the store is part of the contractor's markup.)

If it's you, will you be sure to get just the right piece? Do you have time to sit around and wait for the contractor to indicate when a piece is needed? If you're not there when the piece is needed, does the job stop until you show up?

What If Some Materials Are Broken?

It's almost always the case that during the course of installation, there is some breakage. Who covers it?

If the contractor buys the materials, then the breakage is covered in the markup. If you supply the materials, then you're going to have pay a second time when things break. And when that happens, are you going to get mad and try to subtract the cost of the additional materials from the contractor's bill? No contractor will stand for that.

TRAP

Remember, breakage is always a possibility with any work. If you supply the materials, you are responsible for replacing what breaks at an additional cost. If the contractor supplies the materials, he or she will be responsible, at no additional cost to you.

What If Materials Don't Fit?

Let's say you hire a contractor to put in a sink, which you supply. When the contractor arrives, she discovers that the sink that you bought is the wrong size. Now what happens?

You have to go back and get the right size sink, if one is available. Meanwhile, the contractor has just lost a considerable amount of time.

Even if the sink fits, do you know the right size for all the plumbing connections that go underneath? I know that when I hook up a sink myself, I often buy twice as many fittings as I need (planning on returning the excess), just to be sure I've got the right size when I need it. Even so, frequently there's a part that should fit but that simply won't because the old fittings in the house weren't standard. Now, it's back to the store, once again with inherent delays.

What If Materials Break Later On?

Who's going to guarantee performance? I don't want to pay the installer's price for flooring, so I buy it on my own. Six months go by and the flooring is starting to curl and peel. In alarm I call the installer and demand that he fix it.

But the installer says that it's not the fault of the installation; it's the fault of the materials. So I take a sample piece back to the store where I bought it and complain. Now the supplier says it's not the fault of the materials; they were installed wrong.

In short, I get banged back and forth between installer and materials supplier, each blaming the other and neither willing to accept responsibility for warranting performance. On the other hand, think of how much easier it would be if the contractor supplied the materials. There could be no question whose fault it was, and it would be up to the contractor to make it right.

TRAP

I can almost guarantee you that if you get the materials and labor from two separate sources, when something goes wrong, each will blame the other and neither will take responsibility.

The Bottom-Line Trap

Don't compare what it would cost you for materials with what it will cost the contractor. Remember, built into the contractor's price is the cost of going back to the store for new or different parts and of supplying a warranty. That's the extra you're paying for. (Be sure the contract specifies that the contractor will indeed offer you those services and warranties.)

8

What Kind of Contract Should I Sign?

When you hire a general contractor or a subcontractor, you should have a written agreement. This is not to say that you can't simply do it with a handshake. Many people do. Indeed, I've done it that way myself, particularly when the job was small and well defined, and when I knew the person with whom I was dealing. However, to help avoid problems later on, a written contract is the best way to handle a renovation project.

Why Do I Need a Contract?

The reason you want a written contract is that it puts everything down in writing so that later on one party or the other can't say we didn't know, didn't understand, or thought things were different. It's in writing, spelled out, and if the writing is clear, there shouldn't be any confusion.

A contract clarifies:

- What work is to be done
- When the work is to be done
- Who is going to do the work
- What happens if there's a problem

Further, later on if you end up in small claims court over a dispute with your contractor, the written contract will often be the deciding factor in who wins and who loses.

Where Do I Get the Contract?

The contractor will be happy to supply the contract for you. I've never known a contractor who wasn't ready to whip out a contract for you to sign as soon as you decided to do the work.

However, the contractor's contract might be a single sheet of paper with very little information on it other than the price of the job. That's really too little for you. What you want is much more. What you want is a contract with all the things you need in it spelled out. A good contractor will have a multipage contract ready for you to sign. Read it over carefully.

What If I Want to Make Changes or Use My Own Contract?

My experience with contractors is that even though they may be excellent at the work they perform, often they are not very good at contracts. In other words, they know and understand their own contract, which may have been originally prepared for them by an attorney (or which they may have borrowed from another contractor). They've used it for years, know it thoroughly, and feel comfortable with it.

You whip out your own contract, however, and they'll look at it and wonder if they should sign, or if they should have an attorney look at it. In short, they may suddenly become very suspicious of you. They may hem and haw and finally refuse to sign, saying they'll take it along and have someone else look at it. In short, having your own contract can waste time and even persuade a desirable contractor to refuse to work for you.

On the other hand, from your perspective, you should never use a contract that your attorney hasn't checked out. This applies especially to those generic contract forms found in stationery stores. (They may not include clauses you need or may have clauses that are inappropriate for your job or for your area of the country.)

So how do you come up with a contract that will protect your rights and at the same time not scare away the contractor? My suggestion is that you carefully read over the contract given to you by the contractor to be sure it includes some minimum information.

To be doubly sure, you can tell the contractor you want to hang on to the contract for a few days to think it over. (I can't imagine a contractor not understanding this, since it happens all the time.) Then have your attorney look over the contract before you sign.

What Should Be in the Contract?

The contract should make things clear, not muddy them up. Here are 10 things I look for in any renovation contract I sign:

1. Price. The price should be clearly spelled out. For example, you're having plumbing work done in a bathroom. The contract should specify the total price and what it includes. It might state that a new bathtub is going to be put in. You will supply the tub, and the contractor will install it, including making all necessary connections and dismantling and hauling away the old tub. The total price is $_____.

TIP

Some contracts specify that you will pay separately for all fees such as building permits, plan checks, and connections (to water, gas, sewer, etc.) Check to see whether the fees are *in addition* to the contract price.

2. Payment Schedule. When payment is due should be spelled out. For example, the contractor may want 10 percent upon signing, 30 percent when the job starts, and the balance when it is finished.

TRAP

When a job is finished can be a matter of some confusion. Is it when the contractor says he or she is done? Is it when a building inspector approves the work? Or is it when you say the job is done? A good contract will spell this out.

For larger jobs, a more complete payment schedule may be necessary. The schedule will often specify that certain payments are due as certain work is completed. Here is a typical payment schedule for a room addition.

Payment Schedule for Room Addition

Upon signing	$ 2,000
When foundation is in	5,000
Framing complete	4,000
Rough electrical/plumbing in	2,000
Insulation	1,000
Wallboard in	1,500
Finish work completed	2,500
Work completed	3,000
Retention (30 days)	2,500
	$23,500

TIP

You can create your own completion schedule—for example, the foundation to be finished by July 10, the framing by August 7, and so on. This will help you plan around the work. Keep in mind, however, that many contractors will balk at such a schedule or insist that it be made so loose that it becomes meaningless.

On larger jobs, 10 percent of the cost of the work is typically retained until 30 days after completion. This is done to ensure against defective work that crops up later and also to make sure that there are no problems with mechanic's liens (described below).

3. Start and Completion Dates. As noted earlier, I consider start and end dates to be vital information. I believe that both dates should be specified. However, some contracts state that the work will be "substantially complete" by a certain date. This gives the contractor an edge in case most of the work is done, but a little bit of finish remains. I don't consider such a clause unreasonable.

Contracts for larger jobs may even include a penalty, to be paid by the contractor, in the event the entire job isn't finished on time or (if there is a completion schedule) designated work is not finished on time. For example, for every day the job is late, the contractor will pay a penalty of $500.

Penalties are usually found only on very large, new construction. Most renovation contractors won't hear of them. The reason is that the extent of the work to be done often can't be known until after demolition takes place.

4. The Work to Be Done. Specification of the work to be done should include the following:

- Demolition to be done, including who is to handle removal of debris
- Labor to be done, such as all installation of kitchen cabinets. Specific tasks include hanging cabinets, hanging and adjusting doors, and all finish work.
- All materials to be used. Each material should be specified down to the manufacturer of the product, the model number, and especially the color.
- Cleanup to be done after all the work is completed.

The contract should also contain a statement that everything is to be done in a high-quality, workmanlike manner.

TIP

Be sure to include a statement that new work will match old work as closely as possible. This is particularly important when renovating.

TRAP

Most contracts provide that you, not the contractor, will be responsible for unknown hazards that crop up (such as a sinkhole suddenly appearing in the backyard) as well as for removal and replacement of previous work done without the benefit of a building permit. In other words, if the contractor starts tearing down a wall and discovers wiring and plumbing not up to code, the cost of bringing it up to code will be yours. This provision is only fair, but it is something to watch out for.

5. Who Has Approval? Does the contractor have approval of the work? What about a building inspector? What about you? What recourse do you have if you don't approve the work? Can you withhold the final payment until you do approve? If the contractor refuses to (or can't) make good on work that you find below standard, can you then have someone else do the work and subtract the cost from the contractor's payment? (This is a very good clause to have, since it can save a lot of hassle later on.)

TIP

 You want to be sure you have the right to withhold payment for any defective work.

6. Conditions to Be Maintained During Work. I've found that contractors hate to include a clause specifying "conditions to be maintained." It involves work done while you're occupying the house, a situation that applies to the majority of renovations. The clause specifies that the contractor will use plastic sheeting to protect the areas of the home that are not being worked on, will keep dirt and dust down, will keep noise down by working only during certain hours, and so on. Contractors don't like such a clause because you can very easily hold it over their heads when you have a complaint. On the other hand, you want some assurance that you'll be able to live in the home while work goes on.

Most contracts that do have a "conditions to be maintained" clause will also specify the responsibilities of the homeowner. For example, you're supposed to realize that it is a work site and to watch out for your own safety and that of your family, pets, friends, and anyone else who comes into the home. You're also responsible for protecting your furniture and valuables (best removed before work starts).

TRAP

The stories of contractors who literally drive people out of their homes—by starting work early in the morning or working late into the night, allowing dust to cover surrounding unworked-upon areas, tramping over the home's carpeting with dirty boots, and on and on—are legendary. If you want some protection against all this, spell it out in the contract.

Many cities and counties have specific ordinances with regard to noise and work. Some specify that the work cannot commence, for example, before 7:00 a.m. or continue after 7:00 p.m. You want to be sure the contract specifies that the contractor will follow all the appropriate ordinances.

7. Handling and Charging Changes. Remember from our earlier discussion that you will almost certainly make changes along the way. If you do, how must you present them to the contractor (new plans, written notice, etc.) and how will the contractor charge you for them? Be wary of a charge by time and materials. Instead, look for a new bid on the work to be done so that you can decide if you actually want to go forward with it.

Also, a good contract will specify that the contractor can't change the materials or work without your written approval. If you don't have this clause, you might find that your Italian tile countertop is suddenly formica! (It's not likely, but stranger things have happened.)

8. Workers' Compensation. It should be written in that the contractor will maintain workers' compensation, but be sure you see a current policy. (Remember, you'll also want to be sure you have liability insurance, often a part of your homeowner policy.)

9. Conditions for Terminating the Contract. What's going to happen if either you or the contractor decides that you can't move forward with the work? For example, the contractor starts and you suddenly lose your job. You're in a financial pinch and you want the work stopped immediately. How much do you owe the contractor: the whole amount or only the cost of work completed?

10. Attorneys' Fees and Binding Arbitration. Anything can go wrong, even when both sides have the best of intentions. If it does, and one party sues the other, is the losing party going to be responsible for attorneys' fees? If you win, you'll want the other side to pay. If you lose, you won't want to pay them.

Also, do you want to be bound by arbitration, as some contracts specify? It could save you attorneys' costs. On the other hand, it could keep you from suing if you feel you've been financially injured. Both attorneys' fees and arbitration clauses are something your attorney should help you with.

When Should I Sign the Contract?

Don't be pressured to sign until you're absolutely sure the contract is just what you want. It's too late to reconsider *after* you've signed. Take the time to look the contract over in private and, if needed, to have an attorney check it out. You should be satisfied about the following:

- All the work you want done is included.
- The price is as agreed.
- You're comfortable with all the terms.

TRAP

Be wary of pressure put on you to sign quickly. Sometimes contractors will offer a 5 or 10 percent discount if you sign right away. I've found that even if I wait a few days or even weeks and then say I'll sign, but only if I still can have the discount, I get it.

When Should I Make Payments?

Never, ever pay off the contractor *before* the work is done. If you have a payment schedule, don't get ahead of it. If you have a single payment due upon completion of the job, don't pay it until the work is fully done. Otherwise, you may never get the job completed.

Once, long ago, I hired a painter to completely paint a house that I had built. The cost was around $2500. I agreed to pay $750 up front, to buy the paint, and to pay the balance when the job was completed. But the painter kept coming to me with tales of woe. His wife was sick. The truck broke down. He needed more painting supplies. And feeling sorry for him, I kept advancing money until soon I had paid over $2000, yet the job was barely started.

Then the painter disappeared. I heard he was working on other jobs in the area and eventually tracked him down. He promised he'd get back to work on mine, but never did. By the time I filed suit in small claims court, he had left the area.

The moral here is never pay for work before it's completed. If you do, you might never get the work done.

Mechanic's Liens: What If I Don't Pay?

You may not want to pay because you're unhappy with the way the job turned out. You wanted walnut cabinets and you got oak—because, the contractor says, walnut wasn't available. Or you wanted a seamless granite countertop. But, the contractor says, there's no way to lay down granite without at least one or two seams.

TRAP

When you have a gripe with a contractor, try to work it out. Talk things over and see if some compromise can't be achieved. Perhaps additional work, at no or reduced cost to you, will solve the problem. Or maybe you'll feel assuaged if there is a cut in the price. Don't just refuse to pay.

TIP

If a payment dispute arises and both you and the contractor refuse to budge, you could pay as agreed and then sue the contractor in small claims court to get your money back.

In order to protect suppliers of labor and materials from owners who contract for work and then refuse to pay, every state has instituted mechanic's liens. These allow the supplier of labor or materials (the "mechanic") to place a charge ("lien") on your property.

A lien is technically a money encumbrance that ties up your title. You won't be able to give clear title—in other words, you won't be able to sell or refinance your property—until the lien is paid off. Further, in certain circumstances the lien holder could force the sale of your property in order to recover the amount you owe!

Warning: Mechanic's lien laws are often complex, have strict deadlines, and vary widely from state to state. Check with a local attorney for information on your area.

In short, mechanic's liens are nothing to fool around with.

Who Can "Slap" a Mechanic's Lien on Me?

Anyone who supplies labor and materials to your job can file a mechanic's lien against you. This has some frightening, though rare, consequences. Suppose you hire a general contractor to do the job; he completes it and you pay him. But he doesn't pay his subcontractors. They, then, depending on the state, may be asked to file a mechanic's lien against you and you might have to pay them too. In other words, you could have to pay twice for the same work!

Even if you're your own general contractor, you may pay a subcontractor for work done. But if that subcontractor doesn't pay for the material he or she used, the materials supplier could slap a mechanic's lien on you.

What's the Procedure for Filing a Mechanic's Lien?

Each state prescribes the procedure to be used. In California, for example, there are two parts to a mechanic's lien: the notice and the lien itself.

The notice, also called the "prelim" or preliminary notice, must be served to you before the lien can be filed. In California the minimum time is 20 days after you first receive the material or after labor is supplied. You must physically receive this notice, so most prelims are sent by registered mail with return signature required.

Thus, when you start a job, you may suddenly get a series of pre-lims from materials and labor suppliers. Don't panic! They are just notifying you that if later on you don't pay, they've already served you with notice and can proceed to slap a lien on you.

TIP

Getting a prelim lets you know who is working on your job and supplying materials. The notice can actually help you later when you check to make sure that people were, in fact, paid.

There are time limits for filing a mechanic's lien. These relate to when the job is completed. Generally speaking, you would do well to record a "notice of completion" (you can find one at a stationery store or ask any escrow company to handle it for you). The subs and materials suppliers then have a set period of time to file mechanic's liens (In California it's 30 days; 60 days if you contract directly for the work.) If the liens aren't recorded by then, they will have no effect.

On the other hand, if you don't file a notice of completion, the time limit extends out. In California it is 60 days after work ends or 90 days after the whole project is completed (generally evidenced by a clearance from the building department).

Once the mechanic's lien is filed, the mechanic has a limited amount of time (for example, 90 days) to start judicial action against you. This means the mechanic must file against you (to have your property sold to pay off the lien) in court.

Such filings are rare, since the procedure usually involves an attorney and can be fairly expensive. The threat is enough to make most owners pay up or at least seek a compromise or arbitration.

TRAP

Don't ignore mechanic's liens. Contact the sub or the materials supplier and try to work things out. Often a compromise can be reached. If not, see about arbitration. Once the situation gets to court, it can be very costly.

Are There Problems with Lenders and Mechanic's Liens?

For lenders, the big issue is order of precedence. In other words, which lien comes first?

A mortgage on your property is also a lien, just as is a mechanic's lien. If, however, a mechanic's lien is filed with the county recorder *before* the mortgage is on record, it could have precedence. Consider: You have $50,000 equity in your property; a $30,000 mechanic's lien is filed before a $40,000 mortgage. In a forced sale the $30,000 mechanic's lien would be paid first out of the $50,000 of equity realized from the sale. However, that would leave only $20,000 to pay back the $40,000 owed to the mortgage lender.

Needless to say, the lender would not be thrilled by such an arrangement. It is to avoid just such situations that mortgage lenders demand that their mortgages be recorded prior to any possible mechanic's liens.

The problem is that as soon as work begins or materials are delivered and prelims go out, a mechanic can file a lien on your property. All of which comes down to this: Most lenders won't fund your mortgage if they discover that any work has been started or materials delivered to your property. The lender will insist on waiting until the work has been completed and the time period for filing all mechanic's liens has passed.

Thus, if you need more money to complete the work after the project begins, you may find it impossible to borrow by getting another mortgage on your home. As I said, mechanic's liens are nothing to sneeze at.

What Can I Do to Avoid Mechanic's Liens?

Obviously, you can avoid mechanic's liens by paying your bills. Even more than that, to be sure that you're not being taken advantage of by unscrupulous contractors, you can institute the following procedures to ensure that payment has actually been received.

Get Lien Releases from All Suppliers of Materials and Labor. Typically a contractor will round up all the subcontractors and get them to sign lien releases, then hand the releases to you along with a bill for the work.

TRAP

Unless otherwise specified, lien releases are often conditional. In other words, they release you from a mechanic's lien, provided the supplier of materials or labor gets paid. If you get the release and pay the general contractor and he or she, in turn, doesn't pay the subcontractor, you can still be slapped with a mechanic's lien! Likewise, if your check doesn't clear the bank, you can be hit with a mechanic's lien.

TIP

Get an "unconditional" lien release. Suppliers of materials or labor normally will give you an unconditional release only *after* they have, in fact, been paid (your check has cleared or you pay in cash). The release states that no matter what, the mechanic waives rights to slap you with a lien.

Pay the Labor and Materials Suppliers Yourself. If you're concerned about handing over a big check to a contractor who must then pay subs and materials suppliers, pay them yourself. In larger projects that I have done, I have set up accounts at lumberyards or hardware stores that are billed directly to me. The general contractor has the flexibility to go in and order whatever he or she needs, up to a maximum amount. I get the bill and I know if and when it's been paid. I've had no problem getting contractors to agree to this arrangement.

It's a little trickier with labor. If you're your own contractor, then it will be no problem. You'll know whom you hire and when and if you pay.

If you have a general contractor, then he or she will be less enthusiastic about having you pay subs directly, since the practice undercuts his or her authority. However, if you insist, the contractor may go along.

The real danger is that the general contractor could use subs or materials suppliers without telling you. And, depending on your state, you could be liable.

Use Two-Party Checks.   So-called voucher checks, commonly used in large construction, must be signed by two parties before they can be cashed. Typically the two parties are (1) the general contractor and (2) a subcontractor. By signing, both acknowledge having been paid.

Does a voucher guarantee that the sub has been paid? Not necessarily. The sub can later claim that he or she received only part of the money; you might now have to pay the difference or face a mechanic's lien. It's a less than perfect system.

9

Getting Highly Accurate Bids

Say you were in a car accident (nobody was hurt, thank goodness!) and your auto was damaged. You want it fixed, so you go to a body shop. However, instead of bringing in your car, you just describe the damage. You explain that it was the left front fender, maybe a bit of the grill, and perhaps the hood paint was nicked too. Now you want an accurate bid.

If the repair shop were willing to give you a bid at all, it would be only a guesstimate, such as described in Chapter 4. No shop could provide an accurate bid, or be expected to hold to its bid, because the shop really wouldn't know exactly what the job involved. You'd have to bring the car in.

The same thing happens with a renovation project. You can describe what you want until you're hoarse, but no contractor, sub, materials supplier, or "handyperson" can give you an accurate bid because no one really knows what you want done.

The key to getting an accurate bid is to be able to describe exactly the work you want performed. Anything else and you'll get a bid that's heavily padded, to protect the contractor from the inevitable changes and redesigns.

Of course, if the job is small, you may simply be able to show the bidder what you want. For example, you might walk an electrician through to the kitchen and say you want a receptacle box here and a light box there. Or you might walk the plumber through the bathroom and say you want a sink hookup there. Probably that's all that's needed.

However, if the job is bigger, such as renovating an entire kitchen or adding a room, you should demonstrate what you want in two ways. The first, which we've already discussed in Chapter 6, is by having an accurate plan. The second, which we'll talk about in this chapter, is by providing a detailed spec sheet.

The specification sheet, if it's drawn up properly, will list all the items you'll need down to their size, shape, material, color, and manufacturer. From this sheet, any competent contractor you plan to hire should be able to determine both the scope and the details of what you want. When the spec sheet is added to the plans, you can get an extremely accurate bid.

TRAP

 The accuracy of the bid depends on your not making any changes. As soon as you begin changing either the plans or the specs, the bid is thrown off. As noted in Chapter 8, most contracts provide that if you make changes, the contractor is no longer required to hold to the quoted price.

Whom Should I Get to Bid?

You want only qualified people. That usually means contractors, subs, or even "handypeople" who specialize in the kind of work you want done. For example, you wouldn't call an electrician to put in a sink or a plumber to add a light fixture. Similarly, you wouldn't ask a handyperson to add a room or a contractor to fix a faucet washer. Call the person who is appropriate to the job and who comes with lots of recommendations.

Check back into Chapter 7 for more information on selecting the right person to bid on your job.

How Do I Handle Multiple Bids?

It's important to get at minimum three or four bids. I know that this involves a bit of hassle. It's so much easier simply to take the first bid, particularly if the bidder happens to be a really nice person.

(Contractors and subs usually come across as really nice people, because they know this influences your choice of bids.)

But don't give in just because it seems easier. Go out there and find at least three and hopefully four people to give you bids. Then you'll have a real means of comparison. You could end up saving a bundle of money!

Remember, be sure that each person who bids does so on the same basis. Give each bidder a copy of the plans and the spec sheets. Be sure everyone knows *everything* you want done. Then, when the bids come in, check them over to be sure they involve all the work. It's really easy for a contractor to leave out some portion of what you want done and arrive at a surprisingly low bid. Then, when the job begins and the left-out portion is discovered, the bid suddenly jumps up there to what everyone else's was—or more.

TIP

Talk to the bidders. Make sure they understand everything you want done. Make sure it's in writing as part of the bid.

Also, make sure all the bids are on the same basis. You don't want one bid to be for total cost while another is for time and materials. That's like trying to compare apples and oranges.

What If I Get Wildly Different Bids?

If the bids are all over the place, it means your plans and more likely your specs aren't clear and detailed enough. It means that the bidders really don't know what you want.

Bids for Remodeling Bathroom When Specs Aren't Clear

Bid 1	$14,500
Bid 2	$6,700
Bid 3	$12,850
Bid 4	$9,300

If the bids come in as above, it's time to clarify your plans and specs. More on this topic later.

Bids for Remodeling Bathroom When Specs Are Clear

Bid 1 $13,000
Bid 2 $12,850
Bid 3 $13,300
Bid 4 $13,000

When the plans and specs are clear, the bids should be very close. You may even get two or more identical bids from different bidders.

What If the Price Is Too High?

It often happens that all the bids end up being higher than you expected. What do you do now? You can always get a few more bids. However, if you already have three or four similar high bids, it's unlikely you'll get a top-quality contractor to come in for a lower one.

TIP

When bids are too high, call all the bidders and let them know your problem. Explain what the bids were and stress that it's more than you want to pay. Sometimes, if one bidder is more eager for work at the time, he or she may be willing to cut the bid a bit closer to what you want.

Remember, you don't have to accept any bid. A bid is just an offer to do your work for a given price. Under no circumstances should you feel required to accept any bid if you don't like it.

TRAP

Be wary of any contractor who asks for money before giving you a bid. Coming out, checking your plans and specs, should be free to you, as should the bid. A contractor who wants money up front to do this is trying to lock you in before bidding, a definite no-no.

Should I Try Arguing a Contractor's Price Down?

You certainly can negotiate the price or terms of the contract with the contractor, as noted above. However, if you try to pressure the bidder to come up with a lower price, be prepared for stiff resistance. Most contractors have a really good idea of what their own costs are, and they learned (or should have learned) early in their career the penalties for bidding a job too low.

Further, remember that the contractor deals with bids all the time; you do so only occasionally. Most will have all sorts of arguments to prove that the price they are bidding is reasonable, if not a downright steal, and that the terms are thoroughly fair to all parties. Keep in mind that from their perspective, they may be right! You will need strong, reasonable arguments backed up by facts to change their mind.

TRAP

Be wary of trying to knock a firm price down. When contractors agree to a lower price, they may be calculating that, yes, they'll charge you less, but they'll give you a lesser quality job too. It's better to look for a different contractor who offers to charge less.

Should I Take a Low Bid?

As noted above, if you've done your homework and have prepared a good spec sheet and set of plans, all the bids should be fairly close. After all, the cost of materials is going to be roughly the same regardless of who does the work. The cost of work is likewise going to be similar, unless someone is desperate and cuts you a real deal.

This is why, out of three or four bids, you'll occasionally get one that's way low. You'll wonder whether you should take it or whether it indicates a contractor who's merely incompetent.

When I get a low bid, I first consider the bidder's references and background (see Chapter 7). Is the person a top-quality contractor? Does he or she have a good reputation? If the contractor passes muster, then I always call and talk about the job. I make sure the bidder understands what's involved—that the bid is for all the work, not just a portion.

Finally, if everything checks, I mention that the bid is lower than the others and ask why. More often than not, I learn that the bidder has had a dry spell and is desperate for work. He or she, therefore, is willing to cut a great deal.

If everything else checks out, I go for it, and so should you!

TIP

 Sometimes timing can be everything. Once when taking bids on the foundation and framing of a whole house I was building, I had a contractor submit a bid that was nearly a third less than anyone else's. He had the best reputation in the area. When I asked about the low bid, he said he was between jobs and he wanted to keep his crew working. If he could start work that week, he'd hold to his bid. Otherwise, he'd cancel it. I got him working right away and he did a wonderful job.

How Do I Create a Spec Sheet?

It's not hard to create a spec sheet, but it does take some detail work. Mostly it means you have to finally decide exactly what you want to do. A typical homeowner's spec sheet for a bathroom is shown in Figure 9-1.

When creating your spec sheet, follow these steps:

1. List everything you'll need for the job.

2. List it by manufacturer and model number.

3. When listing wood, nails, and so on, indicate size, quality, and quantity.

4. Indicate any special installation requirements (for example, whether the kitchen sink is a drop-in or is installed under the counter).

5. State that all items purchased by the contractor must meet building code standards in your area. (If you buy the items yourself, you'll need to be specific about code standards.)

Grohe® Euro Plus shower valve

Jacuzzi® whirlpool bath "Builder's Group—Nova"

Panasonic® 11" color TV with white cabinet on pedestal

Flooring vinyl strips—wood colors and texture

Kohler® Portrait Pedestal Lavatory K-2221

Universal Rundle® "Nostalgia" 2-piece toilet #4065-4076

Price Pfister® brass tub drain and overflow assembly

Lithonia Lighting® surface-mounted Tiffany fluorescent ceiling fixture

Price Pfister® roman tub faucet Q06 series

Price Pfister® sink faucet (to match tub)

Common fiberglass showerstall—36"

Built-to-order glass shower door with chrome trim

Built-to-order 36" window, double-pane, safety glass, white trim

Common wood door, white, solid core

Studs—2 × 4 DF

Header—4 × 10 DF

Wallboard—$1/2$", screwed (not nailed—no greenboard)

Figure 9-1 Typical Homeowner's Spec Sheet for Bathroom Renovation

TIP

If you aren't sure of the exact item you want, you can include an allowance. For example, instead of listing a sink, you give yourself a $300 allowance for a sink. You'll fill in the make and model later on.

TRAP

Be sure that the item you want can actually be purchased within the allowance you've set. Sometimes a slight change in shape or even color can bump up the price hundreds of dollars. You'll have to come up with the difference. That's why it's better to check the item out beforehand. (You're going to have to check it out sooner or later anyhow.)

10
How to Deal with Demolition and Cleanup

It's great fun to design a kitchen, bath, skylight, or other project. However, before you devote all your energies to the constructive process, it's important to remember that first you have to take out what already exists. In the best of cases that can be quite a hassle, and in the worst case it can doom your project.

Most people simply make a mental notation somewhere that demolition will be required and then don't bother to think about it again. However, there is nothing that can derail a project as quickly as demolition problems.

There are four areas of concern:

1. The actual demolition
2. Dealing with the mess
3. Unwanted discoveries related to safety: decay, electrical, and plumbing
4. Unwanted discoveries related to health: asbestos and lead

Undertaking the Actual Demolition

The general theory is that anybody can do the demolition. You can hire a laborer or you can do it yourself. All it takes is a sledgehammer and some muscle power. The truth is a little bit different. It all depends on what you are demolishing and what you need to save.

TRAP

If you are working on an historic home, you'll want to save moldings, paneling, and other old pieces. This means that demolition becomes a time-consuming, precise job requiring patience and care. You won't want to leave it to an unskilled person.

In a typical kitchen demolition, for example, you may want to preserve the old cabinets (they can be sold, hung in the garage, or even given away). While the countertop will usually be destroyed (smashed into tiny pieces and carted away, if it's tile), you want to be sure you don't put holes in the walls, break windows, or damage anything that is going to stay. The same holds true with flooring.

In short, before demolition begins, you should identify all the items that are going to remain and then exercise enough care to be sure that they are preserved.

Three Things to Be Wary of When Demolishing

Injury. Be sure that whoever does the work wears protective gear. That usually means—at the least—nonbreakable goggles, heavy clothing, and gloves. (You may also want to consider a hard hat, steel-toed working shoes, and earplugs, depending on the task.) Also use the correct tools. Use crowbars for pulling nails and prying, and sledges for hammering and breaking.

Weight. Don't pull muscles or strain your back. Get help when moving heavy items. Although the tile on a typical countertop may look small, when broken up and put into garbage barrels, it could weight in at thousands of pounds! Other items that can be very heavy are sinks, metal tubs, toilets, windows, solid-core doors, plaster, and wallboard.

Fire. A broken wire can spark and ignite a fire. During renovation, a plumber can start a blaze while soldering copper water pipe. It's not good enough to think that you'll find a pot and fill it with water if there's a fire. Always have a fire extinguisher handy on the job. Get one with an ABC rating that is designed to handle all kinds of fires.

TIP

Clean up as you go. If you're breaking out a plaster wall, have a garbage barrel handy and dump the plaster into the barrel as it breaks off. That will mean one less time you have to lift and carry it.

How to Deal with the Mess

If contractors tell you that they can do renovation work without creating dust, dirt, and mess, either they don't know what they're talking about or they simply aren't being forthright. The mess goes with the job.

However, the mess can be minimized. Good contractors will isolate the work area from the rest of the home. If it's a room addition, sometimes just closing and sealing off a door can be enough. If it's a kitchen or bath, then hanging sheets of plastic floor to ceiling and taping them together can form a fairly effective barrier. However, you should be aware that no barrier will keep out the noise of construction. (Saws, drills, and even hammering can be deafening up close.) And even the best of the plastic barriers may not keep out all the dust and mess.

Can I Live There during the Work?

If you're the sort who constantly cleans up whenever anyone spills anything on the carpet, or who can't stand to see things out of place or a layer of dust on furniture, I'd suggest you move out during the renovation period. It would probably be a whole lot easier on your constitution and frame of mind. That way, when you move back, you'll have only one cleaning job to do.

On the other hand, if you can stand to live in a messy house, with the noise of construction going on at least during daytime hours, then give it a try. It's certainly cheaper than moving out. And you can be on hand to help make decisions when they crop up during the work.

TIP

Be especially careful of children and pets during a demolition and renovation project. Both are extremely curious. And they can easily be unseen and unheard during work, so be on guard against accidental injury.

By the way, count on having to do a major cleanup of your house after the work. No matter what the contractors and work people say about the efficacy of their own cleanup, a safe bet is that you will want to do your own cleaning afterward.

Can I Create a Temporary Kitchen and Bath?

If you decide to stay during the renovation, be aware that you must have a temporary kitchen and bath in the house in order to live there. The building code as well as common sense requires it.

TRAP

Many cities and counties require a working bathroom at all job sites. If you don't have one, you'll probably have to rent one of the "port-a-potties" you frequently see outside job sites. Be aware that these can be fairly costly. Any contractor can tell you how to get one delivered to your site. Check in the Yellow Pages for portable toilets.

If your house has two bathrooms and you're working on one, the other should suffice for your family during the short renovation period. Just be sure that nothing gets down the toilet in the work bathroom to plug up the drains.

If you're doing a room addition, you can typically seal off the work area without any hassle. If, however, you're working on a kitchen, or if the work involves windows or outside walls, it can be more of a problem. With a kitchen, you'll have to either move out or come up with a kitchen alternative.

Kitchen alternatives can be creative. Some people set up a microwave and a hotplate in the garage. This can work if you have a sink in the garage and move your refrigerator in there. Others try to use one of the home's working bathrooms as a temporary kitchen.

TIP

Don't forget that you'll need a refrigerator and sink, a microwave or hotplate, and enough space to store dishes, pots and pans, and silverware in a temporary kitchen.

There are, however, problems with both plans. You need a sanitary surface (countertop) for a kitchen, and garages usually do not have these. So you'll have to come up with something creative.

With bathrooms, the problem is that you have be careful to shut down the bathroom before setting it up as a kitchen. Mixing waste with food preparation can be a prescription for a health disaster. Disabling the toilet and shower/bath in the bathroom during its use as a kitchen is essential.

TRAP

Many building departments frown on using any other area for kitchen purposes, most certainly not a bathroom. Be sure you check this out when you obtain your permits.

If you're doing work on an outside wall, be prepared to seal up the wall at the end of each day. Sealing may include adding plastic sheathing for weather and a fence for security. If the outside wall will be removed or exposed for an extended period, you may want to rethink your own security when it comes to remaining on the premises. (The usual concerns for heating and cooling apply here as well.)

Unwanted Discoveries Related to Safety: Decay, Electrical, and Plumbing

Your project may involve putting new gutters on the home. But, when you get up to the eaves of the roof and begin checking out the wood, you discover that over the years it has rotted away. Suddenly, it's not just gutters that you need, but new eaves, soffits, and more. The cost of the project could easily double in just a few hours of careful evaluation.

You never really know what's behind a wall, ceiling, or board until you remove it. Birds or vermin could have created nests there, adding to decay. There could be wood rot, termite problems, or almost anything else.

All of which is to say, don't assume you know how long or how much a job will take or cost until you've done the demolition.

Never assume that a wall is only a wall. It also can be a conduit for wiring and plumbing. That means when you break into a wall, you're going to stand a very good chance of having to reroute plumbing and wires.

Wiring is probably the easiest to do. However, be sure that any changes you make are up to UBC standards. Also, the codes in different areas vary. For example, some communities require all wiring to be shielded by metal, meaning you'll need to run conduit. Other areas require Romex, or plastic sheathing. And if the code has changed since the original work was done on the wall, you're in for a real hassle.

TIP

If you're rewiring more than 50 percent of the home, the local building department could require you to bring the entire property up to current code. That could be extremely expensive and difficult.

Plumbing can be more difficult. There are two types: potable plumbing for carrying water in and waste plumbing for carrying it out. Typically the waste piping should all be underneath the floors, unless you're on a second floor or higher, in which case the vents will run up through the walls. Potable plumbing is somewhat easier to deal with, since it's usually a matter of soldering copper pipes to connect them all together and directing them around the area you're working on.

With waste plumbing the code is very complex. Something as simple as the angle or diameter of the pipe can be critical, as can the venting. There's also the way connections are made and whether you've got enough "fall" in the line (so that water will run down, instead of stagnate). When "proving" a waste plumbing system to an inspector, you will typically need to put a plug at the lowest point and then fill all the pipes with a column of water to the top of the highest vent. If the system doesn't leak, it'll pass. If it leaks, your entire project (and sometimes a portion of the rest of the house) could get very wet!

All of which is to say, breaking into a wall can be a very challenging experience!

TRAP

Beware of diagonal bracing. Outside walls will typically have a diagonal brace, often a 1"×6" piece of wood or a narrow piece of metal running diagonally across the wall. This keeps the wall from shifting right or left, particularly during hurricanes, cyclones, earthquakes, or other stress periods. If a diagonal brace is in your way, as when putting in a new window, you'll have to remove the brace but compensate for it. The most common compensation is to add a shear panel nearby—a piece of plywood usually ⁵/₈" thick or thicker, several feet wide, cut to the height of the wall, and nailed every three or four inches onto every stud.

Unwanted Discoveries
Related to Health: Asbestos
and Lead

Nearly any demolition carries with it the possibility that you will run into asbestos and lead, especially in older homes. These can be extremely hazardous to health and precautions should be taken.

Lead paint is primarily found in homes built prior to 1978. The older the home, the more likely that lead paint was used. Lead paint could be on the moldings, walls, ceilings, or even the floors. A primary danger is that children will chew on wood covered with lead paint.

Lead ingestion, either by inhalation or by swallowing, can produce all sorts of symptoms, including (at high levels) convulsions, coma, and death. At low levels it can adversely affect the circulatory system, the kidneys, the central nervous system, and the brain. It can cause problems such as hyperactivity, muscle and joint pain, high blood pressure, and loss of hearing.

How Do I Know If I Have Lead
Paint?

Testing for lead paint is fairly complex, although simple tests are available for homeowners. The best approach is to have a technician approved by the Environmental Protection Agency (EPA) come in and test the area of your concern (as well as the entire house). The test costs around $350.

The danger in renovation with lead paint comes when someone tries to remove it. Burning paint off wood can release lead into the air. Sanding lead paint can release lead dust into the air. (Normal vacuum cleaners cannot capture lead dust—special filters must be used.) In short, when the lead paint is disturbed, it becomes a hazard.

TRAP

Encapsulating lead—that is, painting over it—is not considered an acceptable method of dealing with it. The danger is that the paint could chip off or oxidize and the lead could still get into the home environment.

Perhaps the best way to remove the lead is simply to remove whatever it is painted on. Take off the molding and the lead paint goes with it. (Be sure it's properly disposed of.) Remove the wallboard or plaster and the paint goes too.

Generally speaking, specialists (EPA-certified lead abatement technicians) are the only ones who can safely remove lead from a surface. However, anytime anyone is working around lead, that person should wear an approved respirator. Be prepared for the cost. A total home removal of lead paint can cost $10,000 or more!

Asbestos can be much more of a problem. It can be found in floor tiles, sprayed on ceilings, and as insulation material wrapped around pipes (heating ducts as well as plumbing) or lining attics and roofs.

Breathing asbestos can lead to asbestosis, a lung condition that can result in death. It has also been linked to lung cancer and other diseases.

How Do I Recognize Asbestos?

Asbestos is a white material with fibers. But it can be difficult to identify. It can be in solid form, as in vinyl asbestos tile. To be sure, you should have a suspicious area tested. You can gather a sample of the material you are concerned about and send it off to a lab for testing.

For example, you may be concerned about removing floor tiles because they contain asbestos. You can send a portion of a tile in and have it checked. But be sure you send it to an accredited lab. Each state maintains labs accredited for this purpose. A clearinghouse can be found through the EPA (Web site: www.epa.gov/asbestos/index.htm).

The general rule about asbestos is to let sleeping dogs lie. If the asbestos is properly wrapped so that fibers are not breaking off, and if it's unlikely to be disturbed in the future (as when it's wrapped around a pipe in a sealed wall), you may want to leave it alone.

On the other hand, if the asbestos is not sealed and fibers are breaking off—for example, if you are moving floor tiles containing asbestos, or working on ceilings sprayed with asbestos (as was done in the 1970s to create an "acoustical" look)—it's another matter. Anytime asbestos has been disturbed it becomes a serious health hazard.

Again, only technicians specially trained in the removal of asbestos should attempt to handle it.

TRAP

Do *not* remove asbestos yourself. Only if you have been specially trained in its removal should you attempt to get it out of your home. Otherwise, you could make the condition much worse, plus endanger your own life and those of your loved ones.

Removal typically involves sealing off the area so no air can escape to the outside, then installing fans and filters to capture the loose asbestos fibers in the air while workers in protective gear and respirators remove whatever has broken loose.

TIP

Encapsulating asbestos is often considered an acceptable means of handling it.

As a practical matter, a containment policy works well. If I suspect asbestos in floor tiles, for example, instead of removing the floor, with the inherent possibility of releasing asbestos fibers into the air and then paying to have it professionally removed, I will install a barrier (such as plastic sheathing) and lay a new floor over the old. Many times a new floor can be "floated" over an existing floor, thus effectively encapsulating it. The same applies to dealing with asbestos in other areas, such as walls and ceilings, provided the asbestos has not been disturbed. Encapsulation of one sort or another followed by creation of a barrier to keep the area from being damaged is usually the cheapest way out. The alternative—hiring a certified crew to come in and remove the asbestos—can cost more than your entire renovation project!

Don't overlook demolition—it should be calculated into every home renovation job. Don't dismiss the mess—it's an unavoidable part of every home renovation.

11
Can I
Do It Myself?

Why get your hands dirty by doing the work yourself?

The obvious answers are that it's fun and can save you money, sometimes big bucks.

I want to emphasize that fun and savings go hand in hand. But this has a downside few people realize. You really must love doing the work in order to succeed. If, as a homeowner, you do it just to save the money, chances are it will be a long and trying project. On the other hand, if you love doing it, time will fly by and the money saved, though important, will actually seem an added bonus.

Thus the question becomes: How well suited are you to doing renovation work yourself? Is it the sort of thing you really want to and can do? In short, we're going to organize your personal outlook. We're going to find out your "renovation aptitude"!

The Renovation Fantasy

Almost everyone has a secret desire or fantasy. One of the most common that I've observed is the desire to run a successful restaurant. For some reason, almost all of us seem to think that we would make great restaurateurs.

I assume it's the thought of serving truly marvelous meals to other people that's so appealing. Perhaps we see ourselves in a tuxedo or evening dress escorting elegant customers to tables set with fine linen and antique silverware. Or it may be impressing others with our knowledge of vintage wines. Or it may be preparing and serving ethnic meals that we loved as children and now hunger for as adults.

Whatever the fantasy, the reality is almost always jarringly different. The restaurant business is tough and competitive at all levels, and most people who go into it without extensive background, particularly in food service and in financing, fail. Chances are that if one of your secret goals is to be a great restaurateur, you can forget it. The statistics suggest that you will fail at great expense.

To a lesser degree, the same problem prevails in home renovation. Looking at a project, thinking of the money to be saved by doing it yourself, you say to yourself, "Yes, that's just the thing for me!" However, is it really for you?

Remember, a renovation project can involve:

- Hard, tedious work.

- Working with subcontractors and other people you may not particularly like.

- Discovering only at the end of the project that you really aren't able to turn it out as planned.

- Realizing that you really don't have the time to do the work yourself.

I'm not trying to scare you away. I'm simply pointing out that home renovating, like any endeavor, also has a downside. Simply loving the work and anticipating the profits won't cut the mustard. You also have to be prepared for the hard knocks.

How Do I Succeed?

As I noted earlier, the way to succeed in home renovating is to love doing it and to have the skills needed. Below are two self-tests you can take. The first will examine your attitude. Do you really love doing renovating work or are you just kidding yourself? The second will ask you if you have the skills needed. Keep in mind that skills can be learned, but it's very hard to change an attitude.

How Good Is My Attitude?

Your best chance of avoiding most of the problems that home renovating holds, in my opinion, is to be truly suited to doing the work.

I've found that if you are really in it to save money and down deep dislike the task, you'll find a way to fail.

So, test yourself. Figure 11-1 is a simple little quiz that profiles people I have known to be successful in home renovating over the past several decades. Scoring badly does not necessarily mean you will fail. Scoring high does not guarantee you will succeed. This test is simply one additional piece of input to help shape your decision about whether to try home renovating on your own. Remember, the purpose is to give you some insight into what you might face.

The more times you answer yes, the better your chance of succeeding. Scoring: 13 or more checks in the yes column is a definite indication that do-it-yourself renovating is for you; 10 to 12 indicate you'll probably like it; 9 or fewer suggest that you'd be better off hiring it out.

Note that there is no "official" attitude test for determining future success at home renovation.

How Good Are My Skills?

I've always wanted to fly a plane on my own. Someday I'll probably do it. However, I wouldn't advise you to come along as a passenger, at least not at first. Regardless of my desire, I may have no skill at piloting. And until I spend a lot of time cracking the books and taking lessons, I will have little chance of success. In short, simply because I may have the desire or temperament to be a great pilot, that doesn't mean I'll make one.

On the other hand, I've found that people tend to excel at what they have an aptitude for. As an example, mathematicians usually choose that field because they have a natural talent for it and have been rewarded for their talent in the past. Similarly, car mechanics may choose their work not because they studied hard, but because early on they exhibited a mechanical talent. Thus the test in Figure 11-2 just asks what you currently can do well. It assumes that if you can do something well, you have an aptitude for it. Doing badly on the test does not necessarily mean you have no aptitude.

Let's see if you have some of the skills you'll need to succeed at renovation.

As with the aptitude test, there is no set number of correct answers that will guarantee success or failure. However, the more yes answers

	Yes	No
1. Do you like to work with your hands?	_____	_____
2. Do you like to solve problems on your own?	_____	_____
3. When entering an unfamiliar house, are you more interested in how it's built than in the furnishings?	_____	_____
4. Are you interested in architecture and design?	_____	_____
5. If a faucet leaks in your home, do you like fixing it yourself?	_____	_____
6. Do you like planning family projects?	_____	_____
7. Do you enjoy drawing plans?	_____	_____
8. Are you happy explaining, in detail, to other people (such as subcontractors) what you want done?	_____	_____
9. Do you like putting on coveralls and getting your hands dirty working on a project?	_____	_____
10. Do you like negotiating and haggling over prices?	_____	_____
11. Would you rather work on your car or mow the lawn than go to a movie?	_____	_____
12. Do you find it easy to schedule your time on weekends?	_____	_____
13. Do others think that you've done good "handy" projects in the past?	_____	_____
14. Have you always had a secret desire to renovate your home (or a part of it)?	_____	_____

Figure 11-1 Do-It-Yourself Attitude Test

	Yes	No
1. Are you healthy and can you handle moderate manual labor, including some heavy lifting?	_____	_____
2. Do you usually know how things work without being shown?	_____	_____
3. Do you make time to do manual work?	_____	_____
4. Do you work well with colors and patterns, as in paint and wallpaper?	_____	_____
5. Can you handle an electric drill?	_____	_____
6. Can you handle a portable electric saw?	_____	_____
7. Can you hammer a nail in straight the first time?	_____	_____
8. Can you read a set of plans?	_____	_____
9. Can you create a set of plans from which others can work?	_____	_____
10. Do you understand basic home electrical circuits?	_____	_____
11. Do you know about basic home plumbing?	_____	_____
12. Do you understand how a house is built (rafters, joists, walls, floors, roof, etc.)?	_____	_____
13. Have you ever added a wall or window or done other successful and extensive renovating work?	_____	_____
14. Have you ever successfully installed a garage-door opener?	_____	_____
15. Do people consider you a "handy" person?	_____	_____

Figure 11-2 Do-It-Yourself Aptitude Test

you give, the more likely you are to have the skills, and probably the aptitude, to handle a successful job. Scoring: 12 or more checks in the yes column are a definite indication that home renovating is for you; 7 to 11 indicate you'll probably like it; 6 and fewer suggest that you'd be better off letting others do the work.

The Bottom Line

No test can predict your success or failure at home renovating. What these tests can do, however, is challenge you to ask yourself just how prepared you may be for the tasks that lie ahead.

Chances are that if you're now considering do-it-yourself home renovating, you've had some success in building projects of one sort or another in the past; you've already been set in this direction. The two tests should help you decide whether to continue on the path or to think about sitting back on the couch and watching others do the work.

12

Inventorying Your Skills

You may like doing renovation work on your own. You may even have some basic abilities. But what if the job itself requires more skill than you possess?

Can you quickly learn the skills you need? Or are you better off letting someone who's a pro do the work?

Does Hiring a Pro Really Cost More?

First, let's consider what you're actually saving when you do the work yourself. When you're renovating, you usually want to save money because the budget is tight. The question I pose here is whether hiring a professional to do a job really costs more.

When builders hire labor, they must deal with subcontractors, unions, and pay scales. On the other hand, when you hire labor for your small job, you can deal with an individual worker, often one who is doing the job on his or her own time.

For example, I recently needed to have a water heater moved from a kitchen area to a porch. The job involved not only moving the heavy heater but also retrofitting the plumbing to lead out and join the heater on the porch.

If I had found a plumbing company in the phone book and called, I am quite sure that the job would have cost close to $500. However, a friend knew of a plumber who was looking for some work on the side. I got the name and called him. He said he'd do it for $200 plus materials.

Was it worth my time to disconnect and lug a heavy heater across the house, then shimmy through a cramped crawl space and work with old pipe, perhaps breaking it, trying to reroute the plumbing, when I could hire a pro to do it for $200? I hired him on the spot.

Of course, you won't always be able to find an instant "handyperson." Many times you'll have to go the formal route of dealing with a subcontractor, getting bids, and so forth. But sometimes you will come across a deal that makes doing the work yourself simply not worthwhile.

How Do I Find People Who Will Do "Handy" Work?

As soon as you begin renovating, you'll run into people who see your project as a source of a few extra bucks. Mention other aspects of your project (or other projects) and they'll tell you about friends of theirs. Very quickly you'll build a network. Yes, it really does work this way!

What Does It Cost Me to Do the Work?

Always remember that your labor isn't free. It's worth something, sometimes a great deal. The best example I can give is of my own foolishness. About 25 years ago I was renovating a home. In it was a big, old, abandoned refrigerator that needed to be removed. Being young and strong at the time (headstrong, that is), I decided to remove it myself.

I succeeded, at the cost of a hernia, which put me out of action for a month—not to mention doctor and hospital bills. It might have cost me $20 to have someone who did that sort of work for a living haul the refrigerator out. So how much did it really cost me do it myself?

Calculating Your "Wages"

How much is your own work done on a renovating project worth? The temptation is to say it's not worth anything, because it's done in your spare or extra time. Or to say that it's worth so much that you can't put a price tag on it. Both claims are evasions. Your work is worth something and you should be able to figure out how much, or pretty close to it.

The best approach is to think in terms of time, of hours spent, and to calculate what you might otherwise be doing and how much time (and money) you are losing by not doing that other job. Let's say that you're a computer programmer and that you gross about $1000 a week. (You might actually make much more, or less. We're just picking an arbitrary figure.) Your hourly wage is $25.

If you have to take any time at all away from work for the renovation, you should bill yourself at $25 an hour. If you work at renovating in the evening and this causes you to be tired and sluggish at your regular job, resulting in errors or lost time or clients, you should bill that evening's work at $25 an hour. It's taking time away from your regular job in the worst possible way.

The Value of Your Time

Let's say, however, that you do the renovation work only on weekends or in the evening or during your vacation. In other words, you don't really take any time away from your regular job to do it. Does that mean your time is free? I don't think so. There is still a cost involved. If you weren't renovating, could you be taking in other work on the side and making extra cash? Or could you just be sitting on the sofa and enjoying the television?

My own feeling is that although it's difficult to pinpoint the exact value of time spent away from your regular job, that time is still valuable. To my way of thinking, the only realistic way to bill it is at your regular hourly rate. If you are a programmer, even if you aren't taking time away from your work, you are still worth at least $25 an hour.

Thus, we arrive at a working wage for you when you do your own renovation work. The time you put in is worth what you otherwise earn, on an hourly basis, at your regular work.

I'm sure that some readers are thinking that my method of calculating "work worth" is arbitrary and perhaps even unfair, particularly when it comes to extra time. Those of you who feel that way may be right. But I would argue that, if I'm erring, it's probably on the side of not claiming enough!

How much is time spent away from the family worth? How much are you willing to sell your extra time for? Shouldn't it be sold for more than regular time spent at work? After all, aren't you worth more when you work for yourself than when you work for someone else?

My point here is that most people terribly underrate the value of their work. Chances are your time spent on a renovation project is worth far more than you think.

Do I Have the Needed Skills?

Which jobs can you really do as well as a pro, and which jobs require professionally skilled labor? You think you can do everything as well as a professional? You think you can't do anything as well? You may be surprised by what you discover in the remainder of this chapter.

I think that you can learn certain jobs quickly and do them well enough, on the first or second attempt, to get by. A surprising one (to some people) is plumbing. If you're mechanically inclined, you can learn—out of a book—how to do almost any plumbing job required inside a house. Further, in most cases you know immediately if you did it right or not—either it leaks or it doesn't!

On the other hand, some jobs require a lot of skill and training. For example, plastering over sheetrock (plasterboard) is as simple as putting mud (wallboard paste) across a joint. Any child of 10 can do it. However, to do it right so that the wall is smooth and the seam doesn't show takes practice and skill.

If you aren't skilled at taping and texturing, it's well worth the money to get a pro to do it. It's not just the money saved here. It's a matter of getting a finished job that looks good.

Remember, your ultimate goal isn't to save money or even to have fun doing the work. It's to get a good-looking finished product. Do a bad job, and it's eventually going to haunt you. You'll find it far harder to resell your home.

Which, then, are the jobs you should hire out because of the skill level required and which ones should you be able to do yourself? It all depends on your own abilities and experience as well as on how quickly you can learn.

Figure 12-1 is my own inventory, compiled over the years, which may be useful as a guidepost. You may not agree with all my choices, but remember this: The guide is intended to give you direction, not to cast your feet in concrete.

Job	Degree of difficulty for a beginner (1 is easiest; 10 is hardest)
Air conditioner, fix	TTTTTT
Air conditioner, install	TTT
Bath, faucets, install	T
Bath, lights, install	TTT
Bath, plumbing, fix	TT
Bath, sink, fix	TT
Bath, sink, install	TTT
Bath, tile, install	TTTTT
Bath, toilet, install	TTT
Bath, tub/shower, fix	TT
Bath, tub/shower, install	TTTTTT
Bath, tub/shower glass doors, install	TT
Carpet, install	TTT
Carpet, padding, install	T
Carpet, shampoo	T
Carport, build	TTTTT
Carport, design	TT
Ceiling beams, fix	TTTT
Ceiling beams, replace	TTTTTT
Chisel	TTTT
Countertop, install	TTTTT
Deck, cement	TTTTT
Deck, layout	TT
Deck, wood, build frame	TT
Deck, wood, nail flooring	T
Deck, wood, sink post holes	T
Door, handle, replace	T
Door, sliding glass, handle, replace	T
Door, sliding glass, replace	TTT
Doorbell, fix	T
Doorbell, install	TT
Dormer, cut and support roof	TTTTTTTT
Dormer, design	TTTT
Dormer, install	TTTTTTTTT

Figure 12-1 Skills Levels Chart

Job	Degree of difficulty for a beginner (1 is easiest; 10 is hardest)
Drill, electric	T T
Fence, wood, fix	T
Fence, wood, install	T T T
Fireplace, brick, build	T T T T T T T T T T
Fireplace, clean	T T
Fireplace, ready-made, install	T T T T T T T
Fireplace, replace chipped mortar	T T T
Floor, linoleum, install	T T T T T
Floor, preparation	T
Floor, strengthen, straighten	T T T T T T T T
Floor, tile, ceramic	T T T T
Floor, tile, self-adhesive	T T T
Floor, wood, hardwood, even piece, nail	T T T T T T
Floor, wood, random plank, glue	T T T
Floor, wood, random plank, nail	T T T T T T T T T
Furnace, central, installation	T T T T T T T
Garbage disposal, install	T T
Gutters, install	T T T
Hammer	T T
Heater, peripheral, installation	T T T T
House, lift, level	T T T T T T T T T T
Insulation	T T
Kitchen, cabinet, new, install	T T
Kitchen, cabinet, paint	T T
Kitchen, cabinet, refinish	T T T
Kitchen, cabinet, resurface	T T T T T T T T T
Kitchen, dishwasher, install	T T
Kitchen, garbage disposal, install	T T T
Kitchen, light fixtures, recessed	T T T T T
Kitchen, light fixtures, surface	T
Kitchen, linoleum, sheet	T T T T T T T T T
Kitchen, linoleum, squares	T T
Kitchen, sink drain, fix/install	T T T
Kitchen, stove/oven, install	T T T

Figure 12-1 (Continued)

Job	Degree of difficulty for a beginner (1 is easiest; 10 is hardest)
Light fixture, install	T
Paint	T
Patio, brick, mortar	T T T T
Patio, brick, no mortar	T
Patio, concrete, finish	T T T T T T T T
Patio, concrete, pour	T T
Patio, frame for concrete	T
Patio, install wire or steel	T
Plaster	T T T T T T T T
Plumbing ABC, glue, sewer	T
Plumbing, copper, solder	T T
Plumbing, galvanized steel, thread, fit	T T T T T T
Plumbing PVC, glue	T
Plumbing sewer line, dig up, fix	T T T T T
Porch/deck, build	T T T
Porch/deck, design	T T
Porch, screen, enclose	T T
Roof, tar & gravel, redo	T T
Roof, tar-shingles, fix	T T
Roof, tile, fix	T T T T
Roof, tile, replace	T T T T T T T T
Roof, wood, shingles, fix	T T
Roof, wood, shingles, replace	T T T T T
Room, add	T T T T T T T T T
Sanding, electric belt	T T T T
Sanding, electric, rotary	T T
Sanding, electric, rotary—floor	T T T
Sanding, hand	T
Sawing, electric	T T T
Sheet rock, finish	T T T T T T
Sheet rock, install	T T
Sheet rock, nail	T
Sheet rock, tape	T T T T
Skylight, fix	T T

Figure 12-1 (*Continued*)

Job	Degree of difficulty for a beginner (1 is easiest; 10 is hardest)
Skylight, install	T T T T
Slab, cracks, level floor	T T T T
Slab, cracks, patch	T
Spa, install	T T T
Spa, plumbing, fix	T T T
Sprinklers, fix	T
Sprinklers, install	T T
Sprinklers, install automatic system	T T
Stairs, carpeting, fix	T T
Stairs, fix individual	T
Stairs, supports, fix	T T T T
Stove/oven, electric, install	T T T
Stove/oven, gas, install	T T T
Toilet, fix	T T
Toilet, install	T
Wall, block, fix	T T
Wall, block, install	T T T T
Wall, brick, fix	T T
Wall, brick, install	T T T T
Wall, interior, move	T T T T T T T
Wall, interior, remove	T T T T T T T
Wall, plaster	T T T T T T
Wall, siding—exterior, install	T T T
Wall, stucco	T T T T T T
Wall, wood—exterior, install	T T T
Wallpaper	T T T
Water heater, install	T T T
Window, box, install (enlarge wall)	T T T T T T
Window, new, install	T T T T T
Window, replace	T T T
Window, screens, install	T
Window, screens, replace screen	T
Window, storm, install	T T T

Figure 12-1 (Continued)

TIP

 As an individual, you can get a permit to do your own work. But you must usually be the owner-occupant of the property. And you must often be willing to sign an agreement that you will not sell or rent out the property for a period of time (typically six months to a year) after the work is completed. That's so you don't put someone else at risk from your work—if it's going to go bad, it'll likely happen while you're living there!

13
Doing
a Kitchen

According to the adage, the kitchen is the heart of the home. To a great extent, it's true. The kitchen is a gathering place. It's where you will probably spend a great deal of time.

As a result, money spent renovating the kitchen, if it produces a good job, is most likely to return a profit. If there's only one place you plan to do a major renovation, let it be the kitchen.

How Much Should I Do?

Kitchen renovations are usually considered either major or minor. Here's how they break down.

Minor Kitchen Renovation: $3000 to $9000

- Fix broken tile and regrout.

- Paint or restain cabinets.

- Repaint and repaper walls.

- Install new linoleum flooring.

- Replace decrepit appliances and add new sink.

Major Kitchen Renovation: $10,000 to $50,000

- Replace countertop.

- Replace all appliances and sink

- Install all new cabinets.

- Repaint and repaper walls.
- Install new flooring.
- Install new lighting fixtures.
- Replace windows.

Checklist: What Do I Want from a Renovated Kitchen?

To a large measure, what you do will depend on your pocketbook. But, assuming you have sufficient funds, there should be two over-riding considerations when it comes to doing your kitchen. First, what are the norms for the neighborhood? You don't want to over-spend and create a white elephant any more than you want to underspend and create a "cheap-looking" renovation.

Second, how bad is the existing kitchen and what are you going to be happy with? After all, you're going to have to live in the house, so you'd best create a kitchen to serve your needs. To help shape a decision to your present wants and needs, consider the checklist below.

1. *Do you regularly prepare meals in your kitchen or do you eat out?* If you prepare meals, you'll want a kitchen that has lots of countertop space. If you just bring in meals, you'll want more room for a table where you can sit and eat.

2. *How many people in the family are cooks?* If only one person cooks, then you need a relatively small work area. But if several people cook simultaneously, you'll want separate cooking stations.

3. *How many people regularly eat in the kitchen?* Even if you have a large family, people may not all eat together. In that case, a countertop table with high chairs may be useful. If you all eat together on a regular basis, you may want room for a large table and chairs.

4. *How much food do you buy at once?* Some people go out and buy their food for preparation each day. Others buy in bulk and store it. If you plan on storing a lot of food, you'll want extra cabinets and storage space.

5. *Will you have children in your kitchen?* If so, locking cabinets may be a good idea. (Some stoves now have children lockouts.)

You'll also want to consider an outlet for a TV. Perhaps an area for games would be appropriate. What about a surface to accommodate a computer?

6. *Do you use your kitchen as a meeting place?* For some families, the kitchen is the main room of the house. Often people read or study in the kitchen. If that's the case, you'll want as large a kitchen as possible with lots of space for chairs and tables. Perhaps countertop area will be at a minimum. Also, you may want to increase the amount of lighting or direct it over certain areas.

7. *What appliances do you want in the kitchen?* You will certainly want a stove, oven, and sink. What about a garbage disposal and dishwasher, considered necessary in most kitchens? What about a trash compactor, towel warmer, instant hot water delivery system, or built-in microwave? What about built-in countertop items such as a blender and can opener? It's a good idea to make a list of all the items you want in the renovated kitchen so you'll be sure to leave space for them.

8. *What works in your current kitchen? What doesn't?* You don't want to fix something that's not broken. Make sure that any renovation you are planning actually needs doing.

9. *Are you using a workstation triangle?* Placing frequently used items in groups of three works well. For example, having the stove, oven, and microwave together is a food preparation triangle. Having the sink, dishwasher, and countertop space together makes for a cleanup triangle.

10. *Have you checked the traffic flow?* In a renovation you may have only limited ability to change the traffic flow. But, if the current flow is bad, you may want to relocate a door or wall to improve it.

11. *Have you considered safety and efficiency?* You won't want an oven door that opens into a walk area. You won't want a dishwasher door so close to the sink that it bangs your knees when you try to use it.

12. *Have you created a wants list and prioritized it?* The fact is that you probably won't be able to get everything you want in your kitchen because of space or budgetary concerns. So you need to decide what you must have and what you can do without.

TIP

First try to determine how much you should do (given your neighborhood) *without* considering the cost. That way you'll realistically see what needs to be done. Only then figure out how much your budget allows you to do. You may decide that it makes more financial sense to do nothing than to do a half-baked job.

The big three when it comes to doing a kitchen renovation whether major or minor, are:

Countertops (including appliances)

Cabinets

Flooring

Of course, there's more to a kitchen than the above. There's new lighting, windows, and painting. These areas are all covered in separate chapters.

What Do I Do about Countertops?

If you're in an older home, there are only two types of countertops you're likely to have: tile or laminate (such as Formica®). If you have tile, perhaps the tiles are cracked and the grout is discolored. If you have laminate, the surface may be burned, discolored, or worn through in spots, or the laminate may be peeling off. Either way, it may look bad. But you don't want to spend an arm and a leg. Can you fix up the old?

Keep in mind the quality of the home you're in and what is justified by the neighborhood. In a higher-priced area, it may be the norm to have tile, granite, or one of the newer synthetic surfaces. In a lower-priced area, tile or laminate may be the norm. You don't want to do any renovation project that will drive down the quality of the home for its area.

Can I Save the Old Countertop?

If your countertop is tile and it is cracked and banged up, then replacing it entirely is the only solution. On the other hand, the biggest problem with tile is likely to occur around the edges, which take the worst abuse as things get bumped against them. If only a few edge tiles are in bad shape, you may think to yourself that you'll simply replace them and then live with the rest of the countertop.

TRAP

When kitchen tile is old, replacement becomes a problem. Unless you have extra tile in the garage, the chances are remote that you'll be able to go to a store and find the exact same tile in terms of color and texture as in your kitchen. You may be able to find close. But close will look terrible when installed. It will look like a bad job and will create just as much of an eyesore as the original cracked tile.

If any of the edge tile is cracked, I suggest that you replace all the tile on the countertop. Alternatively, you could put an entirely new edge on, if you can find tile that is complementary.

Another solution is to remove all the edge tile and put a hardwood border around the countertop. The hardwood borders, introduced in Scandinavia, are considered fashionable and can add an elegant touch to a kitchen.

On the other hand, perhaps the tile is intact, but the grout is discolored. The situation can be salvaged by using a narrow screwdriver (or other pointed tool) to carefully dislodge the old grout. Try to remove it as far down as you can, if possible to the base, without damaging any of the existing tile. This is a time-consuming and arduous job, and there's always the chance that you'll damage or break loose a few tiles. Maddeningly, this often happens just at the end of the work!

If you're successful in cleaning out the old grout, then regrout the tile. If the old tile is in good shape, regrouting can rejuvenate an entire kitchen.

TIP

If a single tile is loose here and there, you can careful-ly remove it with your fingers or a pencil and then reat-tach and regrout. (Don't use a hard object such as a screwdriver to pry up the edges, which may result in chipping.) The result is often very acceptable.

It is possible to renovate an existing tile countertop without actu-ally replacing all the tile. I have done this, and the results can be spectacular. For more information on installing new tile, check into Chapter 19.

But if you have a laminate countertop that looks bad, simply plan on replacing it. There's really nothing that you can do to salvage it. Old burns won't come out, and faded, worn tops can't be resur-faced. The only thing that can be done cosmetically is to reglue any strips that have come loose from their laminate bond. Usually, how-ever, this is only a temporary fix and rarely looks good.

What If the Existing Countertop Is Not Salvageable?

Before you install a new countertop, the existing countertop must be demolished. This is a messy job that usually requires sledgehammers (in the case of existing tile) to break out the old surface. With other surfaces, such as laminate, it involves unscrewing the counter-top, breaking the seams, and removing the large base pieces. Demolition usually can be done within a few hours.

Then a new foundation (cement, some type of cement board, or plywood) must be laid on the cabinets, and the new countertop placed on top of it. The time frame could be anywhere from a few days to several weeks. You will not be able to use the kitchen during installation of a new countertop.

How Much Will I Recoup?

If you do a good job in replacing a countertop, you should be able to recoup not only all the money you spend but more, sometimes far more.

The reason is simple: As I've said, the kitchen is the most important room in the house. People spend lots of time in the kitchen, and in many respects it is the showcase for the home. Whereas other rooms are just floors, walls, and ceilings, the kitchen has cabinets, appliances, and of course countertops. These show off the quality of the overall home. Often as much money goes into the presentation of the kitchen as into all the other rooms combined.

Renovate the countertop and you will have changed the overall character of the kitchen, presumably for the better.

What's Available and What Will It Cost?

These days a great many different types of countertops are available. They vary in cost quite dramatically, although all of them look very presentable.

TRAP

Be aware that certain types of countertops are in vogue, while others are not. Tile, for example, makes an excellent countertop. However, in higher-priced homes today, it is almost universally avoided in favor of more expensive granite, or one of the newer synthetic tops. Modern laminate also makes a wonderful-looking countertop, because colors and styles can be mixed and matched. However, it is infrequently seen in upscale homes because of the reminder that, in its early days, it was an inexpensive solution. Of course, fashion is fickle, and what's out today could be in tomorrow.

From a building code perspective, it really doesn't make much difference what top you put on the counter. Most codes specify that the top must be nonporous and washable. In other words, food must not be able to permeate the top and decay, producing a health hazard. Therefore, a highly polished surface of almost any kind will do.

For practical purposes, however, there are four basic materials that you're likely to use: laminate, tile, synthetic, and stone. You can install tile or laminate yourself at a considerable savings. There are numerous books available that give you step-by-step instructions. An overview of the procedure for tile installation is given in Chapter 19.

Laminate

Laminate countertop has been popular for at least 50 years. However, don't mistake the old laminate tops you may have seen years ago with their modern cousins. Today's designs are far more colorful, the material is laid down better, the seams can barely be seen, the material is more durable, and the presentation is nothing less than awesome!

Pluses.   Laminate is probably the least expensive countertop. It's often prepared at the factory with sections already laminated to the base; the sections are then quickly assembled in the home, making laminate one of the easiest countertops to install. Alternatively, it can be glued down (the glue is similar to rubber cement) at the site. The surface is hard and easily washable and it's difficult to chip.

TIP

If you decide to install premade laminate tops (with the laminate already glued to the base) by yourself, be careful to get extremely accurate measurements. (You may want to have a professional do the measuring for you.) How the final product looks and how big the seams end up will depend on those initial measurements.

Minuses.   If you put a very hot pan (right out of the oven) on a laminate surface, it could burn, leaving a permanent and unsightly brown or black mark. Also, if the installation is less than perfect, the seams will show and will accumulate unsightly dirt.

Tile

The granddaddy of countertops, tile has been used for millennia. It offers a hard surface that will not be damaged by heat. Tile is basically clay that has been molded into shape, hardened by fire, and often finished with a glaze. Tile countertops are beautiful and have the look of ages about them. They are more expensive than laminate but about half the cost of synthetic and granite (see below). Tile comes in a variety of hardnesses (grouped 1 to 4) and is priced accordingly.

The least expensive tile is around $2 per square foot uninstalled; the sky's the limit from there for truly exotic tiles.

Tile is available from many parts of the world. European, particularly Italian, tile has been in demand for many years. Domestic U.S. tile has improved in recent years to the point where the variety, color, and size are comparable to almost anything available anywhere in the world.

TIP

For a different look, consider Mexican tiles. They tend to be irregular in shape and very colorful. And they are often less expensive than tile from other areas. They produce a distinctive appearance that some people find appealing.

Installation costs vary with labor charges around the country. A good rule of thumb with medium-priced tile is to triple the price of the tile itself for the cost of materials plus installation. Smaller tiles often come attached to a threaded (fiberglass or nylon) backing so that you can lay down a square foot at a time.

Pluses. Tile is versatile. It comes in a wide variety of shapes, sizes, patterns, and colors. It also comes in glazed or unglazed surfaces. (The glaze is the glossy surface that protects the tile.) You can choose between high gloss, semigloss, or low gloss. For kitchen/bath applications a high gloss or semigloss is usually preferred, because it makes the tile impervious to penetration and, thus, to stains. Tile is close to permanent. If applied correctly, it can (and has) remained steadfast for centuries.

Because tile is laid down in pieces, it is relatively easy for a homeowner to install. If you get good instructions, and then follow them slowly and carefully, you can do a good job the first time out.

Minuses. The biggest minus with tile is that the grout tends to get dirty as the countertop is used. Although sealers can be helpful and cleaners can lessen the dirt, the grout tends to be a high-maintenance surface. Eventually, after five or more years, you may find that the dirt is permanent and that regrouting might be the only solution. As noted above, this involves digging out the surface of the existing grout, putting new grout in, and resealing it. It's not a huge project, but it is time-consuming and messy.

In addition, tile can crack and/or chip. A heavy pan slammed onto a tile counter can do major damage. On the other hand, it's relatively simple to break out a damaged tile and replace it with a new one.

TIP

To clean tile, try using a mild solution of hydrochloric acid, the kind that is used to affect the pH in swimming pools. Also, a mild solution of hydrogen peroxide may work well, too. And, of course, there are a wide variety of commercial grout cleaning products available.

Synthetics

Corean® is a new type of surface that has been available for a couple of decades. Corean and other synthetic materials are available in a wide variety of colors and textures, although you cannot easily create patterns with them as you might with tile or even laminate.

Good synthetics cost about twice as much as tile, installed. And you pretty much cannot do the installation yourself, unless you have been specially trained. Professional installation is a wise choice.

Corean produces a look that defines a home as high-quality. Indeed, because of the cost it is rarely found in any but upscale properties.

Pluses. There are no seams at all. A synthetic surface is all of a piece, from one end to the other. It comes in large slabs which, once laid, are glued together. The gluing process is so perfect that it is impossible for anyone but a professional to detect where it was done. The surface is hard and does not chip.

Minuses. Like laminate, synthetics will burn if a hot utensil is placed on them. However, the burn is easy to correct. It is cut out, a piece of the original material is put in its place, and it is reglued. The new surface is as good as the original, and it's impossible to detect where the burn was.

Stone

Stone is currently the most prestigious countertop to own. It is available as natural granite or natural marble (as opposed to synthetic marble, frequently found in bathroom countertops). It is what it says it is: stone from the ground. It is quarried and cut up into three-quarter-inch slabs, which are then cut to fit for the countertop. (Stone tile cut smaller and thinner is also available.)

For years marble was the stone of choice. However, it is porous, and the cost has gone up with its decreasing availability. Granite has become popular in its place. There is, seemingly, no end to the amount of granite available. The colors and textures of granite are more limited than those of marble. However, more and more granite is coming to the United States from quarries around the world; hence the variety of colors and textures is growing.

TIP

 If you want granite, go to the quarry, or the importer. There you'll be able to pick out the exact pieces you want and have them cut to fit. That's the only way to know exactly what color and texture you'll get.

Granite is sold by the linear inch (not the foot), based on a 2-foot-wide (standard) countertop size. Currently the price varies with the quality of the granite, from a low of about $7 an inch to a high of about $25. That does not count the cost to have an edge cut into the granite, which may add several dollars per inch more. (Edges are glued in layers to increase thickness and then cut in a wide variety of shapes.) Also, if you want a deeper piece of granite (more than 2 feet wide), the costs increase significantly. And then, of course, there's the cost of installation, which can add several more dollars per inch. Granite in the form of granite tiles, 1 foot square or less, is also available at a lesser cost.

Pluses. Granite is nature's most perfect countertop. It's been created over millions of years and as a consequence has a hard, generally impervious surface, although it must be sealed. You can drop things on it, bang it, whack it, and unless there's a defect in it, you won't damage it.

Minuses. Your solid granite counter will have a tiny seam where the different slabs of granite have been placed together. Also, if the granite should crack because it wasn't properly laid down, there's nothing you can do except replace it. Laying granite calls for the services of an expert, so you won't want to be doing this yourself.

You must seal granite as soon as it is installed in order to avoid having water and other materials seep into and stain it. And you'll need to reseal it again every few years. This is not a difficult or complicated process, and it takes only a few hours. But you must remember to do it to maintain the surface.

What about the Kitchen Cabinets?

The cabinets are a kitchen's glory—or its shame. Fine wooden cabinets are indicative of an elegant home. Shoddy cabinets with doors that hang badly indicate a run-down house that needs work. Here's another area of the home where it will pay off to spend time and money on. Like countertops, remodeled cabinets should return your full investment and more when you resell. The first question is: Can the old cabinets be saved?

To determine this, you should first give the cabinets a good, fair appraisal. Here's a quick test:

Test to Determine Quality of Cabinets

1. Do the cabinets have an overall modern appearance?

2. Is the quality appropriate for your neighborhood?

3. Do you like their design?

4. Are the doors in good shape and well hung?

5. Are the drawers of good construction and well made?

6. Are the cabinets in good shape overall—not simply worn out?

If you can answer yes to all six questions, then by all means consider keeping your current cabinets and renovating them. Answer no to any question, and consider new cabinets.

How Can I Renovate Existing Cabinets?

There are at three acceptable ways to renovate kitchen cabinets.

1. Paint the cabinets and rehang the doors correctly. This usually involves at least lightly sanding the existing surface. New hardware (handles) should be put on at the time.

TIP

Use oil-base paints when repainting cabinets. The oil base will blend with the stain (or paint) already on the cabinets. Water-base paints will be repelled and will eventually chip or peel.

2. Restain the cabinets. This involves sanding or stripping the existing varnish or paint and then restaining. It should be done only if the cabinets are made of a good-quality hardwood. Use new hardware.

TRAP

Beware of trying to use a lighter stain over an existing darker stain. The result will almost always be a combination of the two, no matter how stripped the wood appears to be. It's better to go darker over lighter.

3. Laminate the cabinets. This involves replacing the doors and then gluing a wood veneer onto the existing cabinet walls. New hardware should be installed.

What Will It Cost?

Typically the cost of painting or staining existing cabinets is well under $2000 for an average kitchen. This should include sanding, applying a primer, and then adding two coats of a final paint or stain (with light sanding after each coat). Consider having the inside of the cabinets painted a matching color at this time.

TRAP

Many people try to save money by redoing the cabinets themselves—after all, it's only "painting." But the stripping and sanding is tedious, difficult work and getting the paint on right can be tricky. Often it's much cheaper in the long run to pay the added cost of having a pro do it.

Laminating the cabinets involves getting special hardwood veneers as well as having new cabinet doors made to order. The cost for materials alone can run into the thousands. A typical kitchen could easily cost around $5000 or more for the whole job.

What If I Go with New Cabinets?

With new cabinets, the sky's the limit. Your costs can range anywhere from a few thousand dollars to tens of thousands, depending on the quality of the cabinets. Figure an additional 15 to 20 percent to have them installed.

New cabinets are often made to order at a shop (sometimes across the country) and are delivered in sections to your kitchen by truck. Sometimes they are already stained or painted, although finish painting or staining may be done at the site. Even though they are made to order, typically you will choose from standard sizes. If you want truly custom-made cabinets, you will usually need to contact a local cabinet maker.

TIP

If you're handy, you can save money by installing the cabinets yourself. It's not hard and takes only one to two days for a typical kitchen. But it is heavy work, requiring lifting the wall cabinets into place and finishing off those areas where the new cabinets do not overlap and extra strips of wood must be added.

TRAP

When installing new cabinets yourself, the key is in buying right. Measure carefully so you end up with the right type of cabinets and the correct sizes. Ready-made cabinets usually come in standard sizes so you can more easily place units next to each other. Be sure to abut the fronts tightly and screw them together. Any spaces or crooked alignment will show badly in the finished product.

What about Flooring?

If your kitchen flooring is more than 10 years old, chances are that some sort of work needs to be done to it. If it's tile, it may need to be cleaned and regrouted (or at least have the grout cleaned). If it's wood, it may need to be sanded, restained, and sealed. If it's linoleum, it may need to be cleaned and polished at the least, and if it's worn or the wrong color or design, replaced.

TRAP

Don't be tempted to put carpeting in the kitchen; even a very tight weave such as high-quality indoor/outdoor carpeting won't do. The reason is that kitchen spills frequently stain. In short order your carpeting will need to be washed, and getting out all the stains can prove difficult, if not impossible.

There are many types of floors available besides wood, tile, and linoleum. Vinyl squares are common. Pergo®, and similar composite wood flooring, holds up very well. Painted cement, though rarely used, has a definite offbeat look. Higher-priced homes may have marble, granite, or slate. These materials are the most expensive you can use, but their appearance and durability are unparalleled.

Linoleum

Linoleum offers a variety of advantages and disadvantages compared with other types of flooring.

Pluses. Although professional installation is usually needed for a good job, linoleum can be laid in one or two big pieces that go down quickly to produce a good-looking result.

Linoleum is one of the less expensive types of kitchen flooring. However, as you move into top-quality modern linoleum, it can become quite costly.

Linoleum is warm to the touch and usually no-slip. You get the greatest variety of color and design of appearance with linoleum.

Minuses. Given the many advantages of linoleum, you might wonder how there could be any disadvantages. There are, however, several.

Many linoleums have a soft surface that can easily puncture or tear. These breaks quickly fill with dirt and show badly. Even hard-surface linoleum is subject to visible and permanent scratches and chipping. Dropping a knife or sharp object can scar the surface. Also, some linoleum wears badly over time. The colors and patterns can fade and can even wear through. Tile, wood, or stone virtually never wears out.

Linoleum has a bad reputation that is largely undeserved. In years past (and to some extent even today) low-grade versions that quickly wore out were the flooring of choice in lower-priced homes. Hence linoleum has become associated with cheap housing. As a result, it is less frequently put into a high-end home.

A Word about "Squares." Linoleum-like tiles made of a variety of materials are widely available in square-foot sizes. Because the tiles are laid down one at a time, almost anyone can do the work and produce a good result. These, too, come in a wide variety of colors and styles.

Squares, however, have a big disadvantage: seams. No matter how well these tiles are laid, the seams around each square eventually fill with dirt and show. Hence, they are almost never used in a high-quality renovation.

Wood

Wood makes an excellent flooring and has been used as such for centuries. Wood floors in many of the older homes on the East Coast are, indeed, generations old. In Japan, wood flooring goes back many centuries.

Pluses.   The advantages of wood are that it provides a durable surface as well as a warm look and feel. A prestige item, wood always makes the kitchen and the rest of home look richer.

Minuses.   Wood has a porous surface that can absorb liquids, causing it to swell and stain. Thus, wood must be properly sealed on a regular basis.

As our forests have been cut down, there simply is less high-quality wood available; as a result, the price has skyrocketed. The labor costs to install wood flooring have increased as well.

As a practical matter, wood is probably not the best choice in a kitchen, since it is susceptible to water damage. However, a host of new synthetics and wood substitutes are available that give the look and feel of wood without its inherent problems.

Tile

Tile has been the flooring of choice for thousands of years. The Romans were renowned for their tile floors. Tile can be found in the most expensive homes in the world.

Pluses.   Tile offers several advantages. It provides a hard surface that, when properly glazed, will not absorb or stain. It is difficult to damage after it has been properly laid (although individual tiles can be cracked or chipped). A prestige item, tile comes in a great variety of colors and sizes.

Minuses.   As with all flooring, there are always some drawbacks. The surface of tile is cold to the touch. Also, tile can be slippery, which is dangerous in a kitchen (although some newer floor tiles have a less slippery surface). High-quality tiles are fairly costly.

Stone

Stone is by far the most prestigious type of flooring. A marble or granite floor speaks eloquently of the quality of the home.

On the other hand, stone is the most expensive flooring. Also, it's cold to the touch, and in some cases the surface can be slippery. Nevertheless, if you want a kitchen floor that shouts elegance, go for stone.

14
Do-It-Yourself Kitchen Projects

Installing a New Sink

Kitchen sinks come in three basic varieties (although there are a host of different sizes and shapes). The surface-mount sink, the type used most frequently by home renovators, has a lip that goes over the top of the counter.

The flush-mount sink butts up against the countertop edge so that it is even with the counter. A special tightening clip holds the sink in place. Finally, there is the under-the-counter sink. It is held in place by clips screwed into the bottom of the counter.

When you don't want to redo the entire counter, install the surface-mount variety. If you do a careful job of removing the old sink, without damaging the counter, you may be able to place the new sink right on the existing lip with no further work to the countertop surface. Otherwise, plan on doing the countertop at the same time as the sink.

TIP

If you're doing a minor renovation, you might be able to save time and money by refinishing the old sink. This involves putting a new surface on it and is best done by a professional. The advantage is that you don't need to remove the sink and tear out the countertop. The disadvantage is that you still end up with the old sink.

What Does a Sink Cost?

You can get a common kitchen sink in metal or in porcelain over steel. Stone and more exotic materials are also available. The cheaper varieties cost as little as $75. From there the price goes up. I have seen a kitchen sink selling for over $1000.

TRAP

Avoid the least expensive sinks, particularly the porcelain-over-metal variety. Usually the porcelain is thin and may chip or wear away easily. Also, stay away from the low-end stainless steel sinks. They easily show water stains. If you're going to the trouble of replacing a sink, get a good one. Expect to pay around $250 for one that's not fancy and is in white.

How Do I Install the Sink?

There isn't a whole lot of skill involved in installing a sink. If it's a flush-mount, you have to make sure it fits the cutout (hole). If it's an over-the-lip model, you have to be sure you have enough lip to hold the sink.

TIP

Always install the faucets before putting the sink in. It's much easier than crawling underneath later on and trying to install them.

A sink that's flush with the countertop or underneath it attaches by means of small screws placed every 4 to 6 inches. A lip sink simply sits on the countertop. Its weight plus some silicone caulk at the edges hold it in place.

TRAP

 Sinks are heavy, sometimes more than 100 pounds. Get help when lifting one into place. Getting a hernia or smashing a countertop is not a way to save money by doing it yourself.

The biggest problem most people have with sink installations is that they never seem to have all the parts at hand. They're always going back to the hardware store for a piece of tubing or some extra drain pipe.

If you plan ahead and cover all contingencies by buying extra parts (particularly for the drain), you'll save yourself a lot of time and headache. The extras can be returned later.

There should be no exceptional problems when installing a sink. Just remember that the sink is heavy and you need to be careful not to drop it onto the counter.

Installing a Garbage Disposal Unit

Today, a garbage disposal under the sink is a must for most homes. It's not that this adds anything to the value of the home. It's just that if such a unit is not there, any buyer will think something is wrong with the property. The absence of a garbage disposal in a modern home detracts from its value. In other words, you simply must have one.

Garbage disposals are readily available at any hardware store. Most units fit standard sinks and drains. You can get an inexpensive garbage disposal on sale for as little as $35. However, the cheaper units tend to have smaller motors and quickly get clogged when any kind of tough material (such as carrots or chicken bones) is sent down the drain. This could result in problems for you down the road.

I always go for at least a $1/2$-horsepower unit. These typically cost between $75 and $100 on sale. They are sufficient to handle most items sent down the drain.

TIP

Don't go for a fancy-looking garbage disposal. Nobody sees it. You just want one that works well. Paying more for a pretty package makes no sense here.

It takes only an hour or so to install a garbage disposal and the skill level required is low. However, installation is tricky, and since you're working under the sink, you'll probably end up with bruised fingers and a couple of bangs on the head.

You'll have to remove the existing drains under the sink and reroute with new drains. (Don't try reusing the old drain pipes, which are probably on the verge of leaking anyway. New pipes cost only a few dollars.)

The new disposal includes a flange and mounting assembly with instructions. The disposal unit is inserted from the bottom and often attaches to a ring that comes down through the hole in the sink.

Be sure to install a new trap (to prevent sewer gases from passing up into the house) and new couplings on all drain joints.

TIP

To avoid any possibility of leaks, install a bead of plumber's putty under the top flange (the part that goes into the sink). Many disposal instructions don't mention this, but instead include a thin paper washer. Don't use the paper washer, it goes underneath the sink; use the putty. It will save you from a lot of leaking problems later on.

From the bottom, the snap ring is usually held in place with three screws. You put it on, twist, then tighten the screws to mount the unit securely. Some disposals, however, have a twist ring that requires you to twist it tight. You'll need a special, wide disposal wrench for this. It's inexpensive and sold in hardware stores.

TRAP

Be sure the unit is securely in place; when it's turned on, it vibrates significantly. If it's loose, the vibrations can cause it to leak.

The garbage disposal will also have a second outlet (actually an inlet) that can be used to connect a dishwasher. If you connect a dishwasher, be sure to knock out the blank blocking the inlet; otherwise your dishwasher won't be able to drain properly.

Installing a Dishwasher

Old dishwashers often get rusted areas inside, especially on the dish racks. Or sometimes they just look old-fashioned. (The newer models are largely digital and look quite elegant in all whites or colors with little chrome trim.) When you do any kind of kitchen renovation such as cabinets, counters, or sinks, replace the dishwasher. It's not that expensive and a new unit can make a big difference to the overall appearance of your kitchen.

TIP

If you want to save the old dishwasher for some reason and the rust and deteriorated areas are just on the racks, try to get new racks. These are available for the more common models. It can be a quick-and-easy solution.

The cost of dishwashers varies enormously. You may be able to purchase a low-end Whirlpool or GE model for $250 or less on sale. On the high end, you could end up spending close to $1000 for an elegant model from the same manufacturer. Other manufacturers offer stainless-steel drum tubs for even more money.

It takes virtually no skill to install a dishwasher. You have to watch out for a few things, however. Be sure you have adequate room

under the counter. The unit fits right under the countertop and usually attaches to the countertop with just two screws. In older units,
there may be additional screws holding the washer to the floor.
Newer models have feet that adjust up an inch or so to help fitting.

TRAP

Be wary of removing an old dishwasher if a new floor
has been recently put into the kitchen. The new floor
may be higher than the old floor on which the washer
sits. You may find the old machine impossible to
remove without breaking the countertop. If you're
installing a new floor, be sure to shim up the dishwasher so that it's level with the new floor and, later on, can
be removed.

Once the dishwasher is in, you may find that you need to install a
tee in the hot water pipe and a shutoff valve in order to supply water
to the unit. The dishwasher needs only hot water, not cold. Also, you
may need to install an electric outlet under the sink, if one isn't
already there.

Be sure that you always include an overflow "air gap," required
by the building code. This is a device that comes up through a hole
in the sink, screws on, and then is capped. Wastewater comes up
from the dishwater to the air gap (preventing backflow) and then
down into the garbage disposal. Should the disposal be plugged,
the wastewater will come out the air gap and flow harmlessly into
the sink.

TIP

You will need to get a permit and have your dishwasher inspected. Almost all building departments require
inspection to be sure that the air gap is properly
installed.

Be sure the unit is level so that it doesn't vibrate when turned on.
Be sure all pipe fittings are tight so water leaks don't develop over

time. Since the plumbing is under the sink, leaks might go undetected for quite a while, damaging or warping your cabinets.

Installing a New Stove/Oven

There is very little incentive to fix old stove/ovens. The cost of new electric burners, for example, is prohibitively high. You can often buy an entire new range for the cost of just two burners! Old gas units, on the other hand, sometimes plug up with grease. The cleaning job is messy, and if the valves are affected, cleanup is difficult. Besides all this, old units look dated. If you're going to renovate your kitchen and replace your cabinets and/or countertop, you should replace your stove/oven as well.

There are all kinds of stove/ovens available. Stand-alone units sell from around $400 to $1500. Drop-in range ovens can be purchased for around $300 to $1300. Wall ovens are about $400 to $800, plus a similar cost for the range top. Some of the nicer units have a glass surface without the unsightliness of individual burners.

Installing a unit requires minimal skill and usually can be accomplished in a matter of minutes. What does take time and skill is creating the openings for them. With the exception of the stand-alone, you'll need to have cabinets and a countertop to accommodate the stove.

The electric units simply plug into a 220-volt socket. If you're putting a unit in an area without such a socket, you'll need to have a 220 line dragged in from your circuit-breaker box. This is a job for a professional, unless you're very competent with electrical circuits. You'll need a dedicated line for an electric stove and oven.

With gas, it's simply a matter of hooking up a flexible gas line to the gas outlet. Be sure to check carefully for leaks.

TRAP

Be wary of installing a gas unit in an area where there wasn't one before. You'll have to drag a new gas line to the area. This requires the work of a plumber, and the installation must be done under permit. Sometimes it's so costly as to make the whole gambit impractical.

When installing a drop-in, be sure that it fits snugly and is screwed in tightly. You don't want it falling out the first time someone opens the oven door!

Installing New Linoleum Flooring

As noted in the last chapter, the big advantage of linoleum over tile or hardwood is the reduced cost (although top-quality modern linoleum can be quite expensive). The appearance can be excellent. Modern linoleum wears well and you avoid the problem of slipping that can occur with some tile and stone floors.

For a novice, however, installing large pieces of linoleum can be very tricky. The hard part is getting them cut to fit the outlines of the floor and dealing with the large, awkward piece of material.

TIP

If you're new at linoleum installation, I suggest you first create a very accurate mask of your floor, a template. Use sturdy cardboard that won't stretch or tear easily. Then place the template of the linoleum in a flat area, such as on a cement garage floor, and make your cuts. That way you'll have a better chance of having the linoleum fit the first time you lay it in place.

TRAP

Laying linoleum flat and then using quarter-round or other finishing wood to cover the ends is the easiest type of installation. Coving or bending the edges up a few inches into the wall can produce a more polished finish and is much easier for cleaning, but should be attempted only by a professional.

The floor must be properly prepared. That means that if it's cement, all depressions should be filled. It should be dry and sealed.

A whole sheet of linoleum is then cut to fit counters, walls, and corners. Then it is glued down.

Certain types of linoleum are rigid and must be softened using a blowtorch. However, too much torching can easily burn them. Other types are very flexible, but tear easily. Also, as noted above, getting the proper cutouts is very difficult with a single large piece, as is making a seam for larger areas.

Once the linoleum is down, roll it. Linoleum rollers are available from equipment rental stores. Rolling spreads out the adhesive and helps ensure good adhesion. Be sure to wipe up any excess glue as you go, since it can become messy very quickly.

TIP

Before going through the hassle of laying linoleum, consider laying individual squares. As noted in the last chapter, they are readily available in a wide variety of colors and patterns. Many come backed with glue, and are easy to cut and to lay down. A pair of scissors, cutting knife, pencil, and cutting guide are really all that is required. Be aware, however, that dirt tends to accumulate and show at the seams. Linoleum squares are never going to look as good as a single laid piece. When laying squares, be sure to draw a starting line near the center of the floor and work out from it. If you start at one side of the room and work across, you may find that your lines are off by the time you reach the other side.

TRAP

With single-piece linoleum or squares, be careful not to get the glue onto the top. It will attract dirt, discolor, and become ugly. It's also fairly difficult to remove. Be sure the squares fit tightly, but not too tightly. If they are forced into place under pressure, they will buckle.

15
Doing
a Bathroom

The bathroom, whether master, main, or guest, is usually the most frequently renovated area of a home after the kitchen. It's a very crucial renovation, because the quality of the bathroom and how modern it is help define the quality (and often the value) of the house. When it comes time to resell, a remodeled bathroom often recoups its cost or more and secures a quicker sale.

When you decide to renovate your bathroom you should address two major issues. First, how much will the bathroom renovation add to the value of the home? Second, how much will the renovation make use of the home more enjoyable?

What Can I Do to the Bathroom?

Bathroom renovations are usually considered either major or minor. Here's how they break down:

Minor Bathroom Renovation: $500 to $3000

- Refinish sink or tub.

- Put on new tub/shower door.

- Add new fixtures to sink, tub/shower, and toilet as needed.

- Paint and wallpaper as needed.

Major Bathroom Renovation: $5000 to $30,000

- Put in new sink, toilet, tub/shower, and extras (towel warmer, etc.).

- Put in new countertop.
- Install new cabinets.
- Install all new fixtures.
- Install new flooring.
- Install new lighting.
- Paint and wallpaper

How Will the Renovation Affect My Home's Value?

As long as you don't overdo it, don't renovate beyond the norms of your neighborhood, you can probably get out all, or even more, of the money you sink into a bathroom, in terms of increased value and quicker resale.

Does that mean you can spend $25,000 on a bathroom and recoup all the money? Probably, if it's a million-dollar house; certainly not, if it's a $125,000 house. The renovation still must be appropriate to the quality of the home.

How Will the Renovation Affect My Enjoyment?

Enjoyment depends on what you want from your bathroom. If you never use a whirlpool tub, why spend thousands installing one? On the other hand, if two of you use the bathroom at the same time, be sure to put in two sinks. You'll use them.

Checklist: What Do I Want from a Renovated Bathroom?

You want to create a bathroom that's particularly suited to your needs, all the while not creating something so weird that it will make reselling the home difficult, if not impossible. The checklist below can help you decide what you want in a bathroom renovation.

1. *Will two people be using the bathroom simultaneously?* If so, you'll need to install two sinks instead of one. In the modern house,

two sinks in a master bedroom have become the norm. One sink in the main bathroom or guest bathroom is still acceptable.

2. *Do you need an additional bathroom in the house?* Sometimes what's needed is not renovating an old bathroom, but adding another one. These days, two bathrooms is considered minimal. In most moderate-priced to upscale houses, at least three bathrooms (master, main, and guest) are considered desirable. (In very upscale homes each bedroom will have its own bathroom.) More than three will enhance the house, but will probably not return much money on the dollar as an investment. Also, expanding families need an additional bathroom, particularly as children become teenagers.

3. *Does the bathroom have enough countertop space?* You may discover that what's really missing is a place to lay out combs, brushes, hair dryers, and so on. Additional countertop space may be all that's really needed in your bathroom.

4. *Is the existing shower, tub, or tub/shower adequate?* It depends on what you like. Some people prefer showers exclusively, others baths, still others a combination. Ideally, the shower is separate from the tub, at least in the master bedroom. There's a safety concern here—a separate shower is easier to get into and out of than a tub/shower combo, since the floor surface is usually less slick.

5. *Is there adequate storage in the bathroom?* You'll need to have space to store toiletries, towels, and linen. And then there are cleaning detergents as well as medications and first-aid items. Each family has different rules about what belongs in a bathroom. If the current bathroom lacks space, you may want to consider additional cabinets.

6. *Does the room need more light?* These days building departments usually insist that there be at least one fluorescent light in a bathroom to give adequate lighting. However, that may simply not be enough, the light may not be where you want it, or you may not like the cool light produced. You may want to add additional directed spot or wall incandescent lights. Not only do these make the room brighter, but their yellow cast makes it warmer.

7. *Are the fixtures of the water-saving variety?* In many parts of the country, water is scarce and getting scarcer. When installing toilets, faucets, and shower heads, you will want to be sure they restrict the flow of water.

Should I Install a New Countertop?

A lot depends on the condition of what's there now. Tile is the most common countertop in bathrooms, with synthetic marble running a close second. Laminate, once a commonly used surface, has declined in popularity over the past two decades. Of course, for upscale homes, stone is in demand.

In older homes, the tile may still be in great shape, since it's less likely to take abuse in a bathroom than in a kitchen. But the colors and style may be old-fashioned or undesirable. If that's the case, you'll want to put in a new countertop.

If the synthetic marble has burn marks, rust, or other stains on it, you will probably want to replace it as well. Although many burns and marks can be removed by sanding, the depressions and rough surface that result can be even more unattractive than the original mark.

Similarly, old laminate usually should be replaced. It may have faded and, if so, is not a feature that will add to the quality of your bathroom.

For the types of countertops you may want to install in your bathroom, revisit the discussion of kitchen counters in Chapter 13. The same materials are used for both areas.

Should I Install a New Sink?

Unless the existing bathroom sink is an antique with high value, always replace it when doing a major renovation. A new sink will add freshness to the bathroom.

TIP

Add a new sink even if you decide to keep the old countertop! Often a slightly oversized surface-mount sink will cover over the area damaged when the old sink was removed.

TRAP

Be wary of metal sinks in bathrooms. They may be fine in other areas of the home, but they lack the elegance needed in this area. A fine porcelain sink is usually a good choice, although (if you can afford it) stone is unsurpassed.

For more information on sinks, check into Chapter 14.

Should I Install New Cabinets?

Cabinets are less critical in a bathroom than in a kitchen. For one thing, there are far fewer of them. The eye sees much more of the countertop, shower, and tub than the cabinets.

You may be able to get by with painting or restaining old cabinets in a bathroom, whereas you couldn't possibly get by with this in a kitchen. It depends on how big a renovation you want to do. Again, recheck Chapter 13 for tips and traps on cabinets.

Should I Install a New Whirlpool Tub?

Before you install a whirlpool tub, consider the following:

- Will you use it?
- Do you have the room?
- Can you afford it?

If you simply replace a tub/shower with a new one, you'll have only the basic chore of retiling or reinstalling a plastic unit. However, if you change the configuration by adding a whirlpool or shower, you'll need to run new plumbing and possibly a new dedicated electrical outlet. In an existing home, that can be difficult and expensive.

TRAP

Beware of adding bathroom fixtures on a slab floor. In order to create a new drain, you may have to raise the tub/shower, cut into the cement slab, or both—a difficult and costly procedure.

Keep in mind, however, that newer homes, particularly upscale models, regularly include elaborate whirlpool tubs. No major renovation is really complete without one.

TIP

Sometimes the existing tub/shower is in good condition, but is covered by a shower curtain only. Installing a sliding door onto the tub/shower combo may be all the renovation that area of the bathroom really needs.

Should I Replace All the Fixtures?

Always put in new fixtures, even in a minor renovation. Replacements include:

- All light fixtures
- Faucets, outlets, and drains on tub, shower, and sink
- Handle on toilet
- Door handle

If you haven't renovated a bathroom before, you will probably get sticker shock when you find out the price of high-quality bathroom fixtures. For a whirlpool tub, for example, a Roman-style faucet can easily cost $500 or more. You could spend thousands on upscale fixtures for the whole bathroom.

On the other hand, you can get durable fixtures for relatively little. A good-quality Price Pfister or Moen low-cost model (these come in a wide variety of prices) sink faucet assembly sells for around $50 to $100. Just remember, however, that people who see your bathroom rarely can tell if you spent $50 or $500 on the toilet or sink. But they instantly can tell a high-quality fixture from a cheap one.

Should I Retile the Entire Bathroom?

Tile is commonly used on floors and walls of bathrooms. When you renovate, the question is whether you should keep the old or go with new.

The answer depends, as always, on the condition and appearance of the existing tile. You will stand to get your money back and more if you replace tile that is:

- Chipped or broken
- Old-fashioned in design or color
- Too low (doesn't come up the wall far enough)

For a high-quality job, and an unlimited pocketbook, you may want to use stone. The goal is always to get a good appearance as well as an efficient bathroom. You want to be able to enjoy it while you live there and to recoup your money when you eventually resell.

What about a New Toilet?

Toilets are strange creatures. We really don't want to spend a lot of time talking about them or even using them, yet they are, in reality, a focal point of most bathrooms.

A new toilet will improve any bathroom. New toilets are available in a wide variety of colors and designs. While a common toilet can be purchased for well under $100, a modern toilet with a striking design can easily cost $1000 or more.

TRAP

If you replace a toilet only, be sure the new one has a bigger footprint than the old. Otherwise, you'll be able to see where the flooring was under the old toilet—and it won't look good at all.

TIP

For an unusual feature in a bathroom, install one of the high-tech toilet seats from Japan. These are cushioned and blow warm air and/or water! They are, however, rather pricey, starting at about $1500.

16
Do-It-Yourself Bathroom Projects

There are many bathroom projects that the average handyperson can do alone. The important thing to remember is that the project needs to be done in a professional manner. That means that it has to work (no leaks) and it has to look good when finished. If either of these criteria is not met, then you're wasting your time doing it yourself.

Most of the work suggested in this chapter is for the master bathroom, which these days has become almost as important as the kitchen as a renovation area. When it's time to resell, most buyers will look particularly closely at the elegance, or lack of it, in these two areas. Of course, there's no reason that these projects won't work equally well in a main or even a guest bathroom.

Installing a Sliding Glass Door on a Tub/Shower

In many homes the tub/shower is closed off by a curtain on a rod. It is true that shower curtains are quite attractive and can add color and design to an otherwise drab bathroom. Even so, many people prefer a sliding glass door. Since the cost of adding the door is relatively inexpensive (usually between $150 and $500, depending on the quality and the design, if any, etched into the glass), and since installation is relatively easy, it's become a favorite beginner's renovation project.

TRAP

Tub/shower doors are readily available from building supply companies. Be aware, however, that almost all ready-made doors are designed for a 5-foot tub. If the area you have is larger or smaller, as may be the case in a custom design, you'll have to get a custom-made glass door, and the cost can be quite high.

The model you get should be appropriate to the house you are remodeling. For example, if you are working on a moderately priced home that has chrome bathroom trim, you will probably want a modestly priced chrome stall door.

On the other hand, if you're dealing with an upscale home that has elaborate cabinets and perhaps even stone around the tub, you will want to get a more elaborate door as well. Keep in mind that it's not just getting a gold or bronze anodized frame that makes for a better-looking door; it's the design etched into the glass. (It goes without saying that you should always insist on safety glass for a tub/shower door.)

TIP

The trend in upscale homes is to have neither a shower curtain nor a door on a tub/shower combo, but rather to have a drain area around the tub sufficiently large that no containment of the spray is necessary. Such a solution, of course, requires a lot of bathroom space.

A tub/shower door is easy to install. It can be done in an hour or two, even by an inexperienced worker. Assuming that the door frame is the correct size, all that's required is to mark and drill several holes into the side walls. Since these walls are frequently tile, a special ceramic cutting drill is used, with plastic fillers added to secure the screws. The bottom is held in position by the side brackets, which are then screwed into place, with caulk being used to give a watertight fit. The top can then be placed on the side pieces and the doors easily hung.

TIP

Be careful when you drill the holes for the brackets; you don't want to crack the tile. Be sure that the grout placed under the bottom sill forms a good seal to prevent water from leaking out. And be sure that the bottom sill is correctly placed—the little holes face inward so water collecting in the grooves will run back into the tub/shower. Finish off with a thin bead of caulk along the inside and outside edges of the sill. To smooth the caulk, wet your finger with water and then run it along the bead. The caulk will smooth out for a professional look. Use a helper to lift the glass doors, which can be heavy. Usually they will require some adjustment at the top to make them level.

Installing a Sink/Vanity

The sink/vanity is the focal point of a bathroom. That's why bathrooms in many upscale homes feature a double sink, with deluxe tile or even stone for the vanity top. It makes an excellent impression. The quality of faucets used with the sink is also critical to the overall look and feel of the bathroom.

TIP

Use the highest-quality materials you can afford in your sink/vanity and that are consistent with the norms of your neighborhood. You'll get a big payback later on when it comes time to resell. Potential buyers will walk in the bathroom and begin "Oohing" and "aahing" over your renovation.

What It Will Cost

The vanity is the cabinet supporting the bathroom sink and countertop. Premade units are readily available from home supply stores. For a really polished look, you can order a specialty cabinet or a custom-made vanity to suit your bathroom. The price difference, however, can be astounding. A premade vanity 5 to 6 feet wide of good-quality construction may sell for under $250. Having one built to spec could cost several times that much.

The faucets are critical in the bathroom. A good faucet can easily run $500 and higher. It's not just that it's better made; it's that it uses more expensive metals. Some of the fancier faucets use gold or platinum plating.

The faucet should match the quality of the house. If a home is in the modest to moderate price range, a good-quality low-cost Price-Pfister or Delta faucet will probably do nicely. But, if the property is truly upscale, you should lean toward a specialty faucet.

TIP

When buying bathroom faucets and fixtures, be aware that many plumbing houses offer closeouts on older models at very deep discounts. Since you need only one or two pieces, you may be able to benefit from these sales. Be careful, however, because many of the top-quality manufacturers also produce loss leaders—inexpensive faucets that bear their name but that do not have the fine appearance or workmanship of their regular line. Be sure that whatever you get, the sink matches the tub/shower.

The installation of the vanity is simplicity itself. Once you get it into the bathroom, use long screws to attach the back supports into the studs. The countertop usually just sits on top and is held in place by gravity, caulk, and the plumbing. It's a good idea to connect the plumbing to the sink before installation, since the small crawl areas underneath make later hookup difficult.

Installation of the plumbing is a little bit tricky. It's easier if you run metal-sheathed flexible tubing to the hot and cold shutoff valves.

TRAP

When connecting the water supply, use either solid tubing or flexible tubing that has a metal sheath. Beware of tubing that has only a nylon sheath. In very cold weather it could stiffen and allow the pipe to burst under changing water pressure conditions. Connect the drain to the drain opening using all new materials.

The work requires a modest amount of plumbing skills. There will probably be no pipe threading or soldering involved. All the joints should be compression fittings and use rubber or plastic washers.

What to Watch Out For

The only problem with the vanity installation is likely to occur in measurement. Be sure the vanity is small enough to fit the space available in the bathroom. Also, be sure that it will get through the bathroom door. You may have to cut a small portion out of the bottom side walls of the vanity to accommodate the baseboard.

The plumbing can be difficult for a first-time renovator. As noted, the easiest approach is to connect the faucets to the sink before you install it. Otherwise, you'll be crawling around underneath trying to get the fittings on.

For the tubes connecting to the hot and cold water, be sure to get hoses that aren't too long or too short. Allow several inches extra for slack. Being way off either way could lead to trouble with the connections.

For the drain, use plastic pipe whenever possible. It's much easier to handle. Today the trap and other drain materials are all available in plastics.

TIP

 If you must connect the water faucets after the sink is installed, be aware of a special offset wrench that fits right up underneath to do the job. Ask at your local hardware store. It costs around $10.

Installing New Faucet Handles

Sometimes the existing faucet handles on the sink, tub, and shower are old-fashioned, caked with paint from remodeling work by previous owners, or just plain rusted, broken, or ugly. Yet, the faucet itself may be in good condition. Ideally, you want to replace the whole assembly; however, in a minor renovation you may simply decide to install new faucet handles.

New handles and spigots are available for most brands such as Delta, Moen, and Price-Pfister. A good hardware will stock many different types. For upscale faucets, you may be able to get new handles by calling the company or checking out its Web site.

Replacement faucets and matching spigots aren't always cheap. However, they will be well worth the cost for the improvement they make.

TRAP

 Many discount hardware stores don't have enough call for manufacturers' parts to stock exact replacements. Instead, they offer "universal" faucet parts. The cost is usually minimal, perhaps under $10 for two handles. Stay away from these. They usually don't fit precisely, but instead must be held in place with a little retaining screw. They may quickly fail with use, and the problem will come back to haunt you; worst of all, they look bad.

Replacing faucet handles is easy and requires virtually no skill. Remove the old handles, usually by lifting a cap on the top and taking out a single screw. Then lift them off and install the new ones.

The biggest, perhaps the only, problem is getting the old handles off. Often rust or mineral deposits have built up, making it difficult to remove them. Since you are going to discard them anyway, you may end up using the claw on a hammer to pry them off. Just be careful you don't damage whatever it is you're using as a wedge against the back of the hammer. Another method is to insert a pair of pliers behind (or under) the faucet to loosen the seat. Then remove the seat with the faucet attached. You can take the assembly to a workshop, where you can use a vise or other tool to pry the old handle off.

Just by putting on new faucet handles, you can spruce up the appearance of a sink, shower, and tub and, thereby, the entire bathroom.

Installing a Toilet

The existing toilet may be old-fashioned, cracked, or stained. It may be either unserviceable or unsightly. Thus, you'll want to replace the entire toilet.

As noted in the last chapter, you can pick up an inexpensive toilet, with all the internal plumbing installed and ready to operate, for under $75. Of course, for that price you get only a minimal unit. Often the toilet is smaller than one you would like, and the flushing action may require more water than many of the new water-saving models. However, this minimal toilet, usually available only in white, is quite serviceable, and many people can't really tell the difference between it and a more expensive toilet.

A deluxe toilet can be quite expensive—as high as $1000 and more—although most cost under $500. Typically these have unusual shapes, colors, and moldings, and their flushing action is excellent.

If you're doing a major bathroom renovation, you will definitely want to consider a deluxe toilet. Keep in mind, however, that the inner workings and handle are frequently not included with the unit, but must be purchased and installed separately. A gold-plated handle alone can cost $50 or more.

Although most people suppose that a toilet is difficult to install, it is actually the easiest of all the bathroom appliances. It is held in place by only two bolts, which attach to the upper flange of the sewer pipe, level with the floor. Simply remove the old toilet, cleaning away all the old wax seal. Put the new one in place, being sure to seat a new wax seal properly and getting the two screws (always use new screws) coming through the holes in the toilet. Then tighten the screws (not too far; you don't want to crack the porcelain).

TIP

 When removing an old toilet wax seal, there's a good chance you'll get some effluent on your hands. To avoid a rash or even a severe infection, be sure to use plastic gloves.

If the tank comes separate, place it on the toilet bowl supports, insert the thick rubber washer in the drain hole, and then tighten the two screws that hold the tank on. For the water supply, use a metal-sheathed flex-hose of the correct length. The entire hookup, barring problems, should take less than an hour.

TIP

 As noted earlier, be sure to measure the footprint of the old toilet. Virtually every model has a different footprint. If you aren't installing a new floor, you want to get a new toilet that has a larger footprint than the original, so that it will cover any rough flooring area. If the footprint is smaller, some of the subflooring may show around the base.

TRAP

 Sometimes the two screws holding the old toilet to the sewer flange are rusted and will not unscrew. Since you are going to dump the old toilet, you may want to cut off the screws with a hacksaw or break the toilet porcelain around the screws, making them easier to get out. If you break the porcelain, watch out for razor-sharp edges that could cut you.

Be sure that the flange from the sewer line, to which the toilet attaches, is in good shape. This flange bolts onto the floor. If it's damaged (so that you can't get new toilet bolts onto it), you'll have to replace it. Simply cut through the line below the flange. Then glue on a union, a new piece of pipe, and a new flange, which you will attach to the floor. With older metal pipe, the procedure is much more difficult and you may want a plumber's help. You'll probably want to convert to plastic pipe, using a pressure clamp fitting over the old pipe. Or you'll have to install a new flange using old cast-iron pipe, tamping in hemp, and then filling with liquid lead. This is a tricky operation and is rarely done today because of the danger of lead poisoning from the fumes.

TRAP

Be sure the toilet bottom is flush with the floor. If it is uneven, tightening the toilet even slightly could cause it to crack. Also, if it is uneven, the toilet will wobble when someone sits on it. When tightening the tank to the toilet bowl, be sure to use the rubber grommets that come with the bolts. They go inside the tank and ensure that water doesn't leak out around the fitting.

Installing a New Tub/Shower

The existing tub, shower, or combo could be cracked or stained with rust, or the fixture simply could be old-fashioned. As a result, you will want to renovate by putting in a new unit.

TIP

If the tub is the only problem, you can resurface the porcelain. This works well and the results are amazing. Tub refinishers are listed in the Yellow Pages. However, check first to make sure there are no major problems with the tile or the drain. If you have to replace the tile around the tub, you're better off replacing the tub as well.

Installing a new tub/shower involves removing the old unit as well as the old tile or other wall coverings and the old fixtures. Also, you may need to go into the wall and floor to install new valves and drains. The job is complex and made more so if you attempt to change the location of the tub/shower. I suggest that, if at all possible, you retain the old position.

Installing a new tub/shower is a major bathroom renovation project. It mostly requires hard work, although many people have the skill to do the job themselves. As a compromise, you may want to hire out the heavy labor part of the job and do the connections (the skill part) yourself.

Often the hardest part of the project is removing the existing tub/shower along with the old tile or other covering. I suggest that you take everything out right down to the studs and base floor. Getting into the wall and floor allows you to replace all water valves and drains, so there won't be any chance of leakage—something you don't want to happen after the new tub/shower is in place. Also, you can check for and correct previous water damage.

TRAP

If your old tub is cast iron, it will weigh several hundred pounds. On top of that, the typical bathroom is only 5 feet wide, and the tub is also that width, so you can't really angle it out. One solution is to use a sledgehammer to dent in the sides of the old tub. This will allow it to slip out more freely. Be sure to wear safety glasses and protective clothing when working with the sledge.

If it's a tub, you'll want to rough in the plumbing, the framing to hold the tub, the wallboard, and perhaps even the new tile. In some cases, the tub is the last to go in. In other cases, the tile or stone is laid down over the edge of the tub.

One solution to a difficult installation is to use a fiberglass tub/shower. These units are readily available at reasonable prices. They even come in several pieces, designed to be installed in existing bathrooms. Be aware, however, that in terms of appearance or value added to the property, they don't hold a candle to a porcelain tub/shower installed with tile or stone.

TIP

If you're installing a faucet and spout, keep in mind that because you're putting in a new wall cover, they do not need to be in exactly the same position as the old. This can be extremely helpful, since the new tub will most surely be different in size from the old one and will require a slightly different location of fixtures.

When removing the old tub, be careful with the drain. Typically an old installation will be rusted, and the drain may break when you try to separate it from the old tub. If it looks like it may break, you may want to cut it a short distance below the tub. A clean cut will be easier to fix with a compression fitting than a long jagged tear, which might result if you try to flex it out.

Fixing Leaky Plumbing

Repairing a leak is actually not a renovation but a maintenance project. However, sometimes just fixing the plumbing helps make the house more livable, so a few words are in order.

Fixing plumbing is a logical exercise. However, it can be dirty and messy and can take some skill, such as being able to solder. If you do it yourself, the materials-only cost is usually negligible. If you call in a plumber, the project becomes quite expensive.

Some jobs, such a handling copper pipe, are fairly easy. However, older homes may have galvanized piping that requires using large wrenches to free old joints and then cutting and threading new pipe. Unless you've done this before, you're better off hiring a pro.

Most water leaks are caused by washers that fail or are defective. Replace the washer and the leak will vanish. Accomplishing this, however, can sometimes be surprisingly difficult and can take an amazing amount of time.

TIP

With leaky faucets, grind or replace the seat (what the washer fits into) at the same time as the washer (Hand-held grinders are available for a few dollars.) The seats get pitted and can quickly wear out a new washer. Grinding or replacing the seat (or the entire mechanism) can keep you from having to redo the job every few months.

If the leak is in the wall or floor, it may be caused by a rusted joint or a burst pipe (usually a delayed effect from a winter freeze). In this case, a section of wall may have to be removed. Or you may have to go into the basement or crawl space or remove a section of ceiling under the floor where the problem exists. For galvanized pipe it usually means unscrewing the pipe (using large pipe wrenches) and, working back from the outlet to the leak, replacing all with new pipe. Copper pipe is much easier to handle. The troublesome section can simply be cut out and a new section soldered in.

In the case of a drain, for plastic pipe a section can likewise be cut out, and a new section glued in. For a metal drain, however, it's easier to cut out the old section and use compression fittings on both ends and then replace the damaged portion with plastic.

For toilets, a wax seal is used under the bowl. Remove the screws that hold the bowl to the floor, and lift. Scrape out the old seal using a putty knife and then press a new seal into place. Refit the bowl to the floor.

TIP

Sometimes a leak in galvanized pipe can be sealed using a metal-and-rubber compression fitting, sold at most hardware stores. The fitting is placed over the break and then screwed into place. It really provides only a temporary solution, however, because the fitting will itself rust out eventually. But for the time being, the leak is gone.

TRAP

Be wary of fixing leaks in tub or shower faucets. To get at the valve, you may have to remove a portion of the wall and accompanying tile. Try, instead, simply to replace the valve stem. The stem unscrews after the faucet handle is removed. A wide variety of replacements are available at most hardware stores.

TIP

When screwing fittings on, try using Teflon® tape or paste. It makes an excellent sealer and allows the fitting to be easily screwed on and, later, unscrewed.

Be aware that when working with old galvanized pipe, you are taking a big risk in creating new leaks. Old steel pipe inevitably rusts inside. Every time you put a plumber's wrench onto it you risk distorting and cracking the metal, causing a new leak. For this reason, I recommend that you use compression fittings when possible and, when not, that you rely on the services of a professional plumber. The headaches avoided are well worth any additional cost!

Bathrooms are not the easiest area of the house to try do-it-yourself renovation, because they are small and difficult to get into. But if done well, a bathroom renovation can make the entire house shine and make you proud of the work you did.

17

Seven Tips When Adding Living Space

Perhaps the biggest renovation project that you can do is to add living space. Maybe you want to add a family room, or an extra bedroom, or even another bath. In order to expand, you'll have to go through many of the steps necessary to build a home from scratch. Here are the typical steps.

Steps to Adding Living Space

1. Collect your ideas.
2. Get a "guesstimate" of costs.
3. Determine how you'll finance the renovation or addition.
4. Make the go-forward decision.
5. Get plans and permissions.
6. Hire the right contractor.
7. Have the land graded.
8. Build the foundation.
9. Frame the addition.
10. Put on the roof.
11. Put on external walls.
12. Install rough electrical, plumbing, heating, and other systems.
13. Install insulation.

14. Finish the inside walls using plaster or drywall.

15. Finish electrical, plumbing, heating, and so forth.

16. Paint and do finish woodworking.

17. Get final inspections.

As you can see, an addition is a major project that shouldn't be undertaken lightly. It can take several months to complete, at considerable cost. Recheck the percentages in Chapter 1 to see whether you'll be likely to recoup the money you invest.

If you're thinking of moving forward, here are the seven most important tips for completing a successful addition.

Get Realistic Drawings

With most renovations, you will want to have at least a sketch to see what your project will look like when it's complete. However, when you add room, you want more detailed drawings. You should get several elevations of the exterior as well as fairly detailed drawings of the interior, especially where the addition connects to the existing building. Yes, this will cost a bit more, but it will be worth the extra expense.

The reason is that you want to create an addition that works with the style and framework of your existing home. Nothing sticks out like a sore thumb more than an addition that is out of balance. Your goal is to create a seamless addition so that a person who doesn't know the home can view it from the outside, walk through the inside, and never suspect that anything has been added. Everything should look like original work—all of a piece.

Unfortunately, this is rarely the case. The trouble is that most people create a home addition only once or twice in their lifetime. As a result, they have no real sense of how the "after" will look just by viewing the "before." The drawings help you visualize what the final result will be, and can help you avoid making a costly mistake.

TRAP

Beware of adding room where it is simply most convenient. Sometimes going up over a garage, or straight into the backyard is the simplest solution. But the results might not look good. Rather, base your decision on what makes the addition an integral part of the home. The quickest and easiest answer may not the best.

Hire a Contractor Who "Speaks" Additions

Not all contractors, not even all good contractors, are created equal. Some are excellent at building homes from the ground up. Others work mostly with interior renovations such as bathrooms and kitchens. But you want a contractor who specializes in additions.

The reason is that adding room is a specialized field. The contractor will need to match the exterior of the addition to the existing home, and that can mean knowing where to find the right materials as well as how to apply them. The contractor will also need to know how to create a complimentary roofline. Then there's matching the interior of the addition. Along the way, the contractor must know how to handle the basics of construction from foundation to framing.

For example, if you're in San Francisco and you're dealing with a turn-of-the-century home, you'll want a contractor who knows where to find, or how to manufacture, the various spindles and ornate woodwork used on exterior walls and trim. The last thing you want is someone who slaps aluminum siding on a Victorian house. (Such mismatching was common up until a few decades ago, when city ordinances stepped in to control the practice.)

TRAP

The older the home, the more specialized the required knowledge. With homes that are 70 or 80 years old, the contractor will need specialized knowledge of construction methods used in the 1920s and 1930s in order to modernize the home to current standards while maintaining much of the original look.

Interview your contractor. Ask for references of previous additions (not just homes built from scratch or interior work). Go to see those projects and ask yourself not only how good the work is but how well everything fits together. Be wary of hiring a contractor who is using you to learn on.

Don't Demolish Exterior Walls Until You've Sealed In the New Addition

The point where the addition joins the existing home is critical. That's where you'll demolish the original wall or door so that you can move between the home and the addition. The tendency is to want to do the demolition as the first step.

Don't. Wait.

Leave the connecting wall or door in place and go ahead and build the addition. In most cases, the existing connection won't get in the way. And it will protect the home from the weather and from the dust and dirt of construction.

Indeed, it's best to hold off as long as possible before demolishing the connecting wall or door. At least finish the new addition's roof and walls so that you won't have to worry about bad weather getting in. If you wait until most of the construction work on the addition is almost completed, you will minimize dust, dirt, and noise.

Ideally, demolishing the connecting wall or door is one of the *last* parts of the project.

Use More Concrete

The foundation of the addition is—well, its foundation. The beefier it is, the stronger and longer lasting the addition will be. However, as in the case of improved electrical or plumbing systems, a better foundation will not bring in more money when it's time to resell. On the other hand, you might not be able to sell at all if the foundation is broken. Also, if you're going to live in the property for a while, you will probably want to do a good job even though you are unlikely to recoup your investment. In this case, a good job usually means more concrete.

If you're adding a room, you'll need at minimum a peripheral foundation (one that runs along the outside edge of the addition). Most foundations (but not all) are made of concrete. Your local building department will specify the type of foundation and its size.

The most common type, a T foundation, actually looks like an inverted letter: ⊥. The footings, at the bottom, are wider than the wall at the top. The building department will specify the depth of the footings and the width. Since T foundations are typically used on flat ground, they tend to be fairly shallow. However, if there is a problem with the soil, such as expansion in wet weather, the footings may need to go deeper.

My suggestion is that, whatever depth and width the building department requires, go a couple of inches wider and deeper. The cost won't be that much more and you will dramatically increase the likelihood of getting a truly strong foundation.

TIP

Use extra rebars (reinforcing steel bars). Rebars are placed in the concrete both horizontally (running with the walls) and vertically at various distances. Typically there will be at least two rebars running along the footings. If the footings are deeper, two levels of rebar may be used. Again, additional rebars won't cost that much more, particularly for a small addition, and will increase the strength of the foundation enormously. Later, even if the foundation should crack, the rebar will keep it in place.

There are many other types of foundation you may need to use, depending on the conditions of the soil. You might want to sink steel pins down to a supporting soil. Or you could use drilled concrete piers (considered better than steel pins) down to a supporting soil.

Many home additions today feature a "slab" or concrete floor rather than a true foundation. Typically a piece of reinforced concrete, four to six inches thick, is poured inside a peripheral foundation to serve as the subfloor for the addition.

TIP

When building on a hillside, use a steplike structure to create a stronger foundation with more support for the addition.

TRAP

Be sure that the mix of concrete is good. When you order concrete from a supplier, you can specify the amount of water, sand/gravel, cement, and additives (various plasticizers). Among other things, the mix will determine how long the cement remains liquid and, hence, workable. However, too much water can weaken the final product. Generally speaking, concrete with less water, which sets up faster, will end up being stronger than concrete with extra water added so that it will set up slower.

TIP

Check the strength of the concrete. When the concrete for a foundation is being poured, samples are placed into special cans (they look like gallon coffee cans). These are typically tested at 7, 14, and 28 days. At the end of 28 days, the concrete should be completely cured to a hardness of at least 2800 psi (pounds per square inch). You'll have to pay a test lab (which supplies the cans) to squeeze the concrete through a hydraulic press to make sure it measures up. In some cases the building department may require this test, but even if it doesn't, you should assure yourself of the quality of the concrete used.

Use More Diagonal Bracing

Nature is an aggressive enemy of the home addition—in almost every part of the country. On the East Coast it's hurricanes. In the Midwest its tornadoes. On the West Coast (and elsewhere) it's earthquakes. In short, whatever you put up, nature in various ways will try to knock down. That means your construction must be as strong as possible. The answer to building strong is often diagonal bracing.

Unfortunately, most first-time renovators have never heard of diagonal bracing. And they certainly tend to overlook its importance.

What is diagonal bracing? Think of it in terms of triangles. Try this experiment. Cut a fairly strong piece of cardboard about a foot long and two inches wide. Bend it in three places. Then fold it to form a square box.

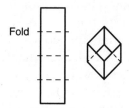

Now try to collapse the box by pushing on any corner. You'll find that with almost no effort, the box collapses on itself.

Next, build a triangle out of the same material using the same technique.

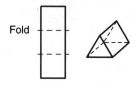

Now try to collapse the triangle. You'll quickly see that it won't collapse at all, unless you distort or crush the cardboard.

The same holds true in building construction. Build square walls (ceilings and floors), and the first time the ground shakes or the wind howls, they may fall over. Build walls that are triangles, and they will hold up to all but the most severe punishment.

But homes are traditionally square, not triangular, so how do you do it? The answer is diagonal bracing—placing pieces of wood or metal at a diagonal to the traditional square building blocks of the home.

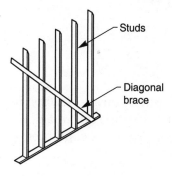

Most building departments specify diagonal bracing. However, usually what they demand is a minimum. And many contractors will often do just that—the minimum. If you want to build an addition that will last, use more diagonal bracing—it's incredibly inexpensive.

There are two basic types of diagonal bracing. The traditional brace is a board, usually a 1 × 6, cut diagonally into the studs on a wall (space for it is cut right out of the studs, then the board is "inserted"). A variation is a metal brace that is placed diagonally against studs and nailed to them. Both methods work well.

Another method is called a "sheer" wall. Here, a piece of plywood, usually ⁵⁄₈ inch thick, is placed up against studs. Then it is nailed to the studs, typically every four to six inches. The stability of the plywood attachment keeps the studs from collapsing as would the box.

Use more diagonal bracing than the building department requires. Use more sheer walls too. For example, whenever you have a part wall between the foundation and the first floor, make sure to apply a plywood sheer wall on at least one side. Whenever you have any length of wall, be sure *all* of it has diagonal bracing.

TRAP

A window or a door on an exterior wall will weaken that wall. Be sure you have diagonal bracing on both sides. If there's not enough room for diagonal bracing (as when a sliding glass door occupies most of a wall), use sheer bracing.

Diagonal bracing is possibly the most underused, yet most useful piece of construction you'll come across.

To Save Money, Do the Plumbing and Electrical Yourself

Electrical and plumbing tend to be the costliest forms of labor in home additions. Of course, if you've got a big budget and don't mind the expense, then by all means hire electricians and plumbers. They can do it faster and easier than you.

But if you're looking to save big bucks, consider doing the work yourself. It is surprisingly easy to master, and you can learn almost all of what you need to know from books. (There are many excellent books out there that teach you the basics of plumbing and electricity—from the Sunset books and other series to individual tomes.)

TRAP

 Some things you need to be shown personally how to do, and once is usually enough. Sweating a copper pipe fitting is an example. It's extremely helpful to see how to clean the pipe, how hot to heat the copper, when to apply the flux and solder, and even how to clean off the excess dripping. Some building supply stores, such as Home Depot, offer free classes in just such things.

You can also save money by handling the heating and air-conditioning ductwork. If you're really handy, you may even want to tackle installation of the air-conditioning unit and the furnace. However, be aware that the work requires specialized tools and knowledge.

Add as Many Windows and Light Areas as Possible

One of the worst (and most frequent) outcomes of a home addition is the creation of dark areas. For example, you add a family room off the living room. In order to do this, one exterior wall of the living room must be sacrificed to become the connecting area between the existing room and the new family room.

Only that sacrificed wall had a window in it. With the window gone, the old living room, and perhaps the new family room, are dark.

To avoid this very common scenario, pay special attention to light when you create additions. You will want to put many windows into new exterior walls, more than you might otherwise think necessary. Also, consider adding skylights to bring light into areas darkened by the addition. These days skylights are better than ever. They don't leak, and they offer a variety of lighting solutions. (See Chapter 18 on skylights.)

If all else fails, add sufficient artificial light to the rooms to compensate for the lack of natural light. Solutions include attractive track lighting, recessed lights, or even lighting hidden in panels.

These seven tips should help you steer a straight course when adding living space. Of course, you may also want to get help on the overall process of creating an addition—from plans to foundation to roof to finishing. For that, I suggest my forthcoming book on building your own home, due out from McGraw-Hill in 2000.

18

Adding
a Skylight

Many homes, particularly older homes, have dark rooms. No, I don't mean the photographic kind. I mean rooms that simply don't have enough natural light.

Usually poor lighting is the result of poor design. A room near the center of the home without much (or any) outside wall will not have sufficient light coming in through windows. Typically bathrooms, kitchens, hallways, and even family and living rooms may be considered dark rooms.

One answer is to add a skylight. It will bring in natural light from outside. In addition, since skylights are "in" these days, it will lend a certain class to the home.

TIP

 Contrary to common belief, modern skylights do not leak. They are made of high-tech materials and, if properly installed, should never allow water in. Older skylights, often hand-made on the spot and not properly sealed, are the cause of the rumor that "skylights always leak."

What Are My Choices?

Today you have a wide variety of options when purchasing a prebuilt skylight.

Energy-Efficient Glass. Many "box" skylights come with double-pane glass that increases their energy efficiency rating. In addition, special coatings on the glass allow natural light to pass through while blocking ultraviolet light. "Low-E" (low-emissivity) coatings can block or increase the amount of radiant energy that passes through the glass, thus helping warm the inside or keep it cool. Also check with the manufacturer for the R rating, which will tell you the insulation value of the glass.

Safety Glass. Tempered glass shatters into pellets rather than shards, thus protecting homeowners if the skylight should break. Though more expensive, it should be standard in home skylights. Laminated glass also works.

Plastic. Many types of plastic skylights are available. These are not the old-style "yellowing" plastic variety. Today's high-tech materials will remain transparent (or translucent) for virtually the life of the house.

Open or Closed Venting. In addition to providing light, a skylight may provide ventilation. Many skylights have a mechanism for opening them from the floor. If your skylight opens, be sure that it has a screen for keeping out bugs and that you can easily access that screen to clean it.

Shades. Sometimes a skylight can let in too much light. This is particularly the case if the skylight faces south. On sunny, summer days the skylight can blast the room with light. You can obtain skylights with shades that close all or a portion of them. Some new high-tech skylights even use electronics to change the glass from transparent to opaque! These, however, are very expensive and are overkill for most homes.

Tubular Structures. Among the newest types of skylights are the small tubular structures, perhaps 10 to 20 inches in diameter, that let in an enormous amount of light. Typically there is a plastic bubble on the roof, then a reflective tube that directs light down into the house, and finally a glass opening on the ceiling that allows light into the room.

Frames. Wood, aluminum, polyvinyl chloride (PVC), and fiberglass—you have your choice of frames for the skylight. What you choose will largely depend on the look you want and the price.

TRAP

Be wary of any skylight that requires painting. Wood, painted aluminum, and vinyl are subject to weathering and peeling. Remember, a portion of the skylight is exposed directly to the elements. Unless you're prepared to spend the time, energy, and money on maintenance, look for a material (such as anodized aluminum or PVC) that does not require painting.

Are There Installation Concerns?

One of the main concerns with installing a skylight is location. Often the place where you want the skylight will have a ceiling that's not close to the roof. In other words, there's an attic in between. There are two basic solutions here. The first is to create a light shaft on the site, with the usual building materials. The shaft, sometimes quite large, connects the ceiling to the roof. It is typically open on the bottom, and the skylight is placed on top. Artificial lighting can be added for the evening. With very large shafts, an attractive ledge can be added around the perimeter on which to place plants or knick-knacks. On the other hand, tubular skylights, noted above, solve this problem easily.

Another concern is that the skylight be properly installed. Many do-it-yourselfers today prefer the flush-mount self-flashing models. You simply remove the appropriate amount of roofing, cut the hole to the correct size, and mount the skylight right on top. The flashing, used to keep out water, comes with the unit and you replace the roofing material right on top.

The less expensive edge- or curb-mounted models require that a curb be built onto the roof to accommodate the skylight and that flashing be manufactured on the site. Professional installation is required.

If the skylight is not properly installed, it will indeed leak. For that reason professional installation is recommended. However, a do-it-yourselfer who purchases a flush-mount self-flashing unit and follows the instructions carefully should not have problems.

TRAP

Beware of installing skylights on tile roofs. The roofs themselves are fragile and simply walking on them incorrectly can result in breaking the tiles.

TIP

Some homes do not have attics. Rather, there is roofing on one side of the rafters, insulation in between, and ceiling on the other side. In such cases an attractive look can be achieved, without disturbing the structural integrity of the roof, by leaving the rafters in place. Simply have the skylight installed on the roof, remove the ceiling and insulation, and block the space between the rafters. Having the rafters exposed below the skylight offers a very modern look. (Just be sure to use a sealed skylight. An open one would expose the rafters to excessive weathering.)

Also, when framing a larger skylight, be careful not to weaken the roof by cutting rafters. This is particularly important if your roof has snowload requirements. Whenever possible, insert the skylight between two existing rafters. If the space is too narrow, you'll have to cut one beam and strengthen the remaining rafters before framing the skylight box. In a big job, always check with an engineer on how best to best construct the box and strengthen the remaining rafters.

A final installation concern is the weather. It should go without saying that when you have the skylight installed, pick a day when no rain is forecast. You don't want to have a hole cut in the roof just as it starts pouring. It's always amazing to me that installers seem oblivious to the weather. They're often so confident that they can get the job done quickly (and they don't get paid unless they're working) that they start a skylight project when the weather is threatening. Put your foot down and don't let work begin unless the sun is shining.

19
Tiling

Tile has been used for floors, walls, countertops, and even ceilings for thousands of years. It was one of the few building materials in the ancient city of Pompeii that survived the eruption of Mt. Vesuvius in A.D. 79—proving just how durable a substance tile is.

Expert tile installation is widely available and compares very favorably with installation of stone, plastics, and laminate. It can be done quickly, with a minimum of waste (since unused tile can usually be returned). If properly installed, tile creates a very professional and neat-looking finish. Also, even if you've never laid tile before, if you're careful and take your time, you should be able to come up with a fairly good result the first time.

There are a wide variety of tiles available. Some are quite reasonably priced; others have prices that will take your breath away. Most tiles are glazed to increase durability and improve appearance. The exceptions are certain Mexican and quarry tiles, which have a more natural surface.

Tile is rated according to its use and its ability to resist water. Vitreous tiles, generally considered impervious to water, are available in limited colors and styles and are most commonly found on floors. Various grades of nonvitreous tiles are used on walls and countertops. These tiles can be sealed to keep water out.

How Do I Decide Which Tile to Use?

There are several criteria you will need to consider.

Cost. While your eye may lead you to some exquisite tile, your pocketbook may lead you away. When calculating costs, be sure you take into account the trim pieces, which often cost more than all the flat tile put together.

Appearance. Tiles are available in a variety of colors, and range in size from 1-inch pieces to square-foot pieces and larger. Often smaller tiles are attached by a fiberglass backing to create larger square-foot sections.

TIP

Use small tile in small areas, such as bathrooms and countertops. Use large tile for large areas, such as floors. Use colored tiles sparingly, since they can easily overwhelm the other features of a room.

Availability. Not all tile is always available. Further, even though the flat tile may be available, the trim pieces you need may not be. Be sure to check what you can get before you make your decision to purchase.

Nonslip features. Some tiles are less slippery than others. Extra grit may be added to the surface to increase slip resistance.

Assembling the Tools and Materials You Need

Line up all these tools before you begin:

- Buckets
- Chalk line
- Clean rags
- Diamond-blade electric wet saw (for bigger jobs)
- Framing square
- Level
- Nipper

- Rubber gloves
- Rubber mallet
- Safety glasses
- Snap cutter
- Sponges
- Straight edge
- Tape measure
- Notched trowel (for adhesive)
- Rubber-faced trowel (for grout)
- Utility knife

Be sure to buy all the pieces of tile you may need beforehand. It will save many trips back and forth to the store. As noted earlier, if you buy extra, most stores will let you return what you don't use.

To lay the tiles, you'll need a good adhesive. The generic name for tile adhesive is "thinset." Premixed adhesive (which is not really thinset at all) is called mastic. It is the easiest type of adhesive to apply, but forms the weakest bond with the tile. Mastic shouldn't be used for floor tiles, since it has no give when dry and any movement of the floor could cause it to come loose.

True thinset is cement with a wide variety of additives to make it more flexible and last longer when wet. Usually it's mixed with water—the more water, the weaker the ultimate bond. Epoxy in the form of resins and hardeners can also be mixed in to strengthen the bond, but they are difficult to work with because of their short drying time.

You will also need to decide on the color and texture of grout for your tile. Grout can be either rough (with lots of sand in it) or smooth (with mostly cement). Grout isn't added until the tile has been laid and set.

TIP

If the grout is the same color as the tile (or close to it), it will give a more formal look. If the grout is a contrasting color, the appearance will be more dramatic and casual.

How Is Tile Installed?

Tile installation depends on whether you are working with counter-tops, walls, or floors.

Installing Tile on Counters

When counter tiles are installed, a substantial portion of the work will involve the edges. You'll probably want to use some sort of specialty trim. Edge tiles are available in a great variety of designs, from V-cap to bullnose. However, not all tile designs have all possible trim. Be sure to make sure that any trim design you choose is available for your tile color and style.

TIP

Cut as few tiles as possible. The fewer the cuts, the easier the laydown and the better the final appearance. Try not to cut pieces smaller than half the size of a full tile. They end up looking as though you were trying to cover up a mistake.

TIP

Avoid awkward small-tile areas, particularly around sinks. Be sure that the cut tiles on one side of a sink are the same size as those on the other. Always position the cut edge of a tile near the wall, not at the tip of the counter.

TRAP

When measuring a countertop, first calculate the space required for the trim pieces. Only then measure how much room you'll have available for the flat tile.

Using wood trim instead of tile on countertops creates a Scandinavian look that is much admired in some corners. If you go this route, be sure to leave only as much space between the wood and the first row of tile as you do between any two rows of tiles. You may have to cut through the wood base of the counter to trim the top in order to make the border fit. Also, be sure that there is a way to anchor the wood border. Use brass screws if possible; if you just nail in the border, it may later separate from the counter. Finally, be sure that the wood border is no higher than the surrounding tiles and that you stain the wood *before* you grout; if you don't, the chemicals in the grout will discolor it.

Installing Tile on Walls

The biggest problem with walls is that they are almost never perfectly straight. At the corners, that means that one wall will not be plumb with another. It may be up to an inch out of line at the top, bottom, or even middle.

TRAP

"Greenboard"—wallboard that has been treated to prevent fungus infestation—has long been used in wet areas such as bathrooms. The problem, however, is that greenboard is more easily susceptible to water damage than is regular drywall. If it gets wet, it's likely to cause rippling, bubbling, and crumbling. Don't use it as the moisture from the thinset could weaken it.

As with countertops, be sure to put the cut pieces toward the inside—near the corner of another wall—not at the edge of the work area. Always use a level to be sure that the tiles remain straight.

TIP

When tiling walls in a small area, such as a bathroom, always start with the largest wall first. Also, you may want to straighten the walls before beginning. It will save you an enormous amount of hassle later on.

TRAP

Be careful when installing tile onto drywall. Yes, you can do it, but the drywall must be firmly secured to the studs behind it. Don't rely on drywall nails; use long drywall screws instead.

Installing Tile on Floors

The big decision is whether to go with the existing floor or to rip it up. The safe answer is to rip up the floor down to the bare boards or concrete. However, if the existing surface is solid with no give or sway, you may be successful in laying new tile right on top of it. You can often save a lot of time and money in the process. Tile will stick to almost any dry, clean surface. (If you try laying tile on top of linoleum or old vinyl flooring, be sure to sand the surface so the adhesive will have something to grab onto.)

TRAP

Be suspicious of existing floors in bathrooms. Almost always there will be some water damage or rot. A good idea is to rip out the existing floor down to the subfloor in a bathroom just to be sure you've got a solid, dry, fungus-free surface.

Ten Steps to Laying Tile

The procedure for laying the tile is fairly straightforward. Follow these steps.

TIP

It's always helpful to lay a few tiles down on the floor or counter beforehand to see how they'll look. Don't be afraid to set out a large patch. Better to decide now, before you use adhesive, that you don't like the look than after it's cemented down.

TRAP

Dirt will always do you in. Be sure to vacuum the surface thoroughly before you begin. Carefully remove any greasy spots.

1. *Prepare the base.* Like the foundation of the house, the base of the tile must be solid for it to stand up over time. Generally speaking, whatever base you choose should be solid, dry, and smooth. A mortar base is generally considered best for counters, since it can be precisely leveled. However, plywood and "wonderboard," a cement/fiberglass composite, will do as well. You can even use drywall, with certain precautions as noted.

TRAP

Before putting a plywood base on a countertop, be sure that all the cabinets are securely attached to the wall and to each other. If the cabinets shift, they can cause the plywood to move up or down or even separate at the seams, resulting in cracks in grout or even in the tiles.

A mortar bed is actually several layers thick. It can begin with a plywood base, followed by cement that is leveled. Next comes a waterproof membrane (to prevent moisture from coming up from the bottom and dislodging the adhesive). A pattern-wire base is often added for strength. The top bed of mortar is placed above it, followed by the thinset adhesive and then the tiles. Thus:

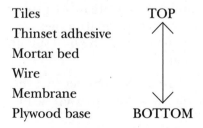

Tiles — TOP
Thinset adhesive
Mortar bed
Wire
Membrane
Plywood base — BOTTOM

2. *Lay out the work lines.* When doing countertops, start with the sink and draw a line widthwise across the counter in front of it.

If there is no sink, draw a line at the edge of the trim tile. This will be your horizontal work line. (Draw the line boldly right on the surface.) Then draw another perpendicular line to help you keep the tiles straight as you move forward.

When doing walls, start at the center of the most prominent feature, such as a tub or sink. Then draw vertical and horizontal guidelines on the wall. When doing floors, start near the center of the room. Draw a straight edge wall to wall. This is your lead line. Draw another line perpendicular to it. This is your secondary line. Follow the lines with the tile.

TRAP

 Avoid the temptation of starting at an edge of the floor, counter, or wall. You may save some cutting of tiles, but you probably will not end up with straight lines or a balanced look—both of which are far more important on tile surfaces.

3. *Apply the adhesive.* Use only as much thinset (cement adhesive) as you can cover with tile in a short period of time. Too much adhesive can dry out before you get to it, requiring a nuisance cleanup. Use a notched trowel with the notch sizes recommended by the manufacturer of the adhesive. Test the adhesive to be sure it's ready for the tile. Lay a trial piece of tile down and then pull it up. It should come up with adhesive uniformly across its back.

4. *Lay down the tiles.* Be sure to leave room for the grout between them. Plastic spacers are a good aid here, but be sure to remove them after the adhesive dries and before you lay the grout. When laying tile down on a countertop, start with the trim tiles and try to avoid dragging the tile across the adhesive; do the backsplash last. When doing floors, start at the center.

5. *Shape the tiles using a cutter and snips.* Remember that the center is the easy part. Most of your time will be taken up at the edges, where you have to cut tiles to fit.

6. *Secure the design.* Move the tiles lightly on the thinset to get them just where you want them. Let the tiles set up for half an hour,

or whatever period the manufacturer recommends. Then come back and tamp them with a rubber mallet. This helps the adhesive set up and stick both to the base and to the tiles. (Don't tamp hard; you don't want broken tiles!)

7. *Clean up.* Remove excessive adhesive from the surface of the tiles. Let the tile adhesive set up (usually 24 to 48 hours).

8. *Mix the grout.* Use water sparingly. Let the grout "slake" or set up for at least 10 minutes. Then apply the grout using a rubber trowel. With a downward diagonal stroke (at a 45-degree angle to the tile), push grout into the grooves. Be sure to get as much off the surface of the tiles as possible.

TIP

The grout between the tiles should have a nice concave shape rather than bulging out. The way to accomplish this is to remove some grout from the groove, stopping just below the surface of the tile. Usually, the first time you try it you'll think you're removing too much grout. Chances are you're not.

9. *Clean the tile.* Let the grout sit until it begins to harden (sets up). Then clean the surface with a damp sponge. Don't leave too much water in the sponge, since that will dilute or remove the grout.

10. *Let the grout cure.* When a film forms over the tile (after about half an hour), remove it with a clean cloth. It will rub right off.

TIP

If you're going to use a tile snapper (a device that scribes a line on the tile, then breaks it into two pieces), practice on some flat tile first. The snapper takes some getting used to. Be sure to use a pair of tile nippers for round or difficult cuts. Have the bullnose trim cut on a diamond wet saw (available for rental at many building supply stores). You can't afford to make mistakes on trim tile with a snapper.

Plan on going slowly. Even professional tile workers can take days to install tile. Just remember that this is a sequential process—you put in one tile after another. As long as you're careful that each piece fits where it's supposed to, you should come out okay. Trying to hurry makes for a terrible job.

20
Replacing Doors

Many homes, particularly tract homes, are built with inexpensive doors, both exterior and interior. Translate that into "cheap-looking." You can upgrade your home very quickly by adding new doors.

Replacing Front Doors: Making a Good First Impression

There are 55 million homes in America that are over 10 years old. More than half of these are over 20 years old. And where the age really shows is in the front door.

It doesn't take a whiz kid to realize that one of the first areas to consider renovating is the front door. After all, it creates the first impression that anyone coming to your home will get. If the doors in your residence are new and, more important, stylish, they will say much about you and your home.

On the other hand, if the doors are old-fashioned, tattered, ill-fitting, and unattractive, they will also speak volumes about you and your home. That's why front doors are often the first place to begin renovating.

What's Involved?

Replacing a door is not as simple as taking the old front door off its hinges and putting in an attractive new one. Often new doors won't fit. You may need to change the frame that the door sits in. Then there's the whole matter of hinges and handles.

TRAP

A great many homes built more than 10 years ago have double front doors, each about 30 inches wide—a trend that was fashionable at the time. Today, however, a single front door, 36 inches wide, has become the rule, and it is increasingly difficult to find the older, narrower double doors. You can special-order them, but at considerable cost.

Replacing a front door can easily cost $1000 or more, substantially more. And it's not the sort of work that the average homeowner can do. Getting the door to fit right in its jamb with proper insulation so that it doesn't leak cold (or hot) air into the house is no mean feat.

How Much Will I Recoup?

You will probably get back every penny you put into a new front door and more. It's one of the few renovation projects that often actually recoups more than a dollar for every dollar spent.

The reason is that the door is the face of your home. It's really the first thing that people look at up close when they come in. If you're reselling, the front door sets the tone for the buyer. A rich, elegant front door says the home is rich and elegant. An old, worn front door says the home is old and worn.

TIP

When it's time to resell, remember that the front door is the first thing a buyer not only sees up close but touches. And, as everyone know, first impressions are critical.

What's Available and What Will It Cost?

Today front doors come in a whole host of materials as well as a great variety of prices. However, you want to pay attention to price here and not be penny wise and pound foolish. An inexpensive front door may subvert your intention of making a good first impression.

Metal Doors

Metal doors are a high-tech product that has been widely used in recent years. Usually they come in a variety of surface designs and some even have glass inserts, usually at the top.

Metal doors are not really metal through and through. Rather, they are composed of a metal skin that has been wrapped around compressed wood, or a metal skin into which has been pumped any of several foam-type substances. Usually the metal itself is steel, which comes painted with a primer, ready for you to paint.

The big advantage of metal doors is that they do not warp and they provide high energy efficiency, something that is greatly desired in areas where the temperatures drop well below freezing. Also, they are one of the most inexpensive door designs currently out there. You can buy metal doors, on sale, for under $100, and a couple of hundred dollars will yield you an attractive design. This is the reason metal doors are preferred by builders.

TRAP

 Metal doors can be dented. And once that happens, it's very difficult to remove the dent. (The process is sort of like fixing a dent in a car fender.) Also, a metal dent can rust, making the door very unattractive indeed.

The big disadvantage is that metal doors are usually prehung. You can't shave a quarter inch off the bottom if a door doesn't fit.

Wooden Doors

Without doubt the most attractive doors are made of wood. If you want to add value to your home, add a wooden door, particularly one with glass inserts.

TIP

Glass inserts in a wooden door may not be energy-efficient. They let cold air in during the winter and hot air in during the summer. If you want a door with glass inserts, try to keep them as small as possible. Very attractive narrow inserts on the door or at the top can provide beauty while reducing heat loss.

Currently the most favored of the wooden front doors are made of oak. The luxurious look simply is hard to match in other woods. Running in second place are doors of mahogany, birch, and fir. They offer appeal in a variety of different shades.

Although wooden doors can be purchased prestained, normally you'll want to have them stained after they are hung. (You can then sand out and finish any minor damage caused by the hanging process.) Staining can be done professionally, or you can do it yourself. It's not hard, doesn't take long, and usually produces outstanding results. (See Chapter 21 for more information.)

TIP

Be sure to get a solid-core front door. It's wood product all the way through. The door is heavy and difficult to batter down, thereby offering a lot of security.

Many front doors are actually a veneer of wood (such as mahogany) with a filling of foam or pressed wood. In this sense, they are as high-tech as metal doors. Filled wooden doors can be engineered not only for appearance but for energy efficiency, warp resistance, and strength.

TRAP

Any wooden door is going to be susceptible to moisture. Thus, while you might expect a metal door to last virtually forever, a wooden door will need to be refinished occasionally (possible as often as every few years). The door will also be susceptible to warping.

Doors made of solid oak, walnut, mahogany, and other scarce woods are very expensive. It is not uncommon for such doors to cost $1000 and more, uninstalled.

Fiberglass Doors

Recently introduced, fiberglass doors are an attempt to combine the best features of wood and metal. They typically have a fiberglass outer skin that has been molded to look like wood grain. The doors can be painted and, to some degree, stained to make them appear to be wood.

Fiberglass doors are more energy-efficient than metal and slightly more costly as well.

What about Installation Costs?

You can pretty much figure that it's going to cost you several hundred dollars, at minimum, to have a new door installed. Some door suppliers will hang doors for a percentage of their cost, against a minimum price. For example, the minimum price for a prehung door might be $150, with a 15 or 20 percent cost increase for more expensive doors. Hanging a door from scratch adds to the cost.

To save money, don't special-order a door. There are a great many door manufacturers, and each has dozens if not hundreds of designs. Typically, however, a showroom will have only a couple of styles on display, and may have those models in stock. If you buy what's in stock, you can often save half or more off the full special-order price. Of course, what you gain in savings you lose in choice.

Install prehung doors yourself. First remove the old door and jamb. Since the new unit includes the door on its hinges, the jamb, and the insulation, there's no real "hanging" involved. The only trick is getting the door lock or handles in place. You can always hire a handyperson to do that if you're not sure how.

A best bet is to spend the money to have a professional install individual doors. It's a project that looks disarmingly simple. Yet it takes great skill to get the doors on their hinges and working correctly.

Get a prehung door. The hinges are already in place, as are the framing and weather stripping. It's easier and cheaper to install.

What Extras Do I Need?

Hinges.   If the door is prehung, it will come with hinges. If not, you'll need to buy new ones.

Hinges come in solid brass, steel, and steel plated with brass. The most expensive, and best, are the solid brass hinges, but they do cost more. (They may discolor from oxidation, but can quickly be cleaned up. But they won't rust or fail to function properly in cold weather.)

TRAP

Don't think you can reuse the old door hinges. Just discard them. Typically they will be the original, brass-plated hinges installed when the home was built. If they show any rust at all, you can be sure of the plating. The hinges may be sprung and usually aren't worth playing with.

TIP

Always use more hinges rather than fewer. Three hinges at minimum on a front door, four if possible, will help prevent warping.

Hardware.   A wide variety of door fixtures are available. Solid brass is highly attractive (and expensive), but you will have to spend time cleaning the parts. I prefer brass-plated steel. Yes, they may rust out in time, but they are so much less expensive than solid brass that after five or ten years you can afford to replace them. Expect to pay $75 and up for the hardware. (Lower-end products tend to rust, are usually more difficult to install, and do not look particularly attractive.)

Be sure to get both a door lock and a deadbolt, for security. You get what you pay for here. Typically the more you spend, the more quality and security you get. I once bought a home on which the previous owner had installed a $10-type door lock. One day I misplaced the key and didn't want to break an expensive window to get in, so I decided to break the door lock. One swing from a hammer sent it flying and the door opened! So much for inexpensive locks.

TRAP

Some manufacturers offer deadbolts with keys for both inside and out. Besides being a terrible idea, it may be illegal in some areas. If there is a fire and you don't have the inside key, you may not be able to open the door and escape.

Viewer.   A viewer, sometimes called a peephole, is not a necessity, particularly when you have glass panels in a door. However, it is a plus where security is a concern. It typically costs around $5.

Side Panels.   If you're replacing two 30-inch doors with one 36-inch door, you'll need two 12-inch side panels. These should match the door and often come with their own glass inserts. Side panels for both or just one side are widely available.

TRAP

You can often buy side panels either as separate items or as part of a prehung door set. Go with the prehung. It is far, far, far easier to install and the results are usually more eye-appealing.

Weather Stripping.   If you get a prehung door, all the weather stripping should be included. If not, you'll have to install it in addition
to the door. Be wary here. The procedure is not always that easy. It
can be particularly difficult to get the weather stripping to lay right
so that the door closes easily yet maintains a tight fit.

Changing Interior Doors

In most houses, interior doors are hollow-core, meaning that they
consist of a wood frame with flat veneer glued on the front and back.
As a result they are lightweight and, quite frankly, flimsy. Typically
the veneer surface has been either stained (if it's neutral wood) or
painted.

You can easily switch to solid-core wooden interior doors, which
come in a wide variety of styles and are readily available in standard
indoor sizes. You can purchase an excellent interior wood door,
unpainted and unstained, for around $150. (By contrast, a hollow-
core door costs as little as $30.)

Unless you are experienced, you are best off getting a prehung
interior door, with hinges already attached to the jamb. Again,
remove the existing door (by punching out the hinge pins) and
then use a crowbar to remove the jamb and surrounding molding,
being careful not to damage the wall on either side.

Once the old door is out, you fit the new one into the jamb and,
using wood shims (available where the door is sold), set it in place
and then nail the jamb in. Finally, put on new molding (unless you
were careful enough to save the old).

TIP

Don't overspend on interior doors. While replacing
them will add to the value of the home, it won't add
much. More than anything else, the new doors simply
lend an indefinable (but real) elegance to the interior.

The entire replacement process shouldn't take more than a few
hours; once you get good at it, you'll need much less time than that.

Changing Sliders

Many homes come with sliding glass doors leading out to the patio or backyard. After a time, the metal wheels on the sliding door wear out and it becomes hard to move. Further, the metal itself can date a house. The usual course of action, therefore, is to replace the doors.

You can replace sliders with wooden, metal, or vinyl doors. A recent trend is to install French doors, the kind with lots of small windows.

A standard replacement slider for a 5-foot door can cost $200 or $300. Change that to plastic and the price goes up $100. Move on to wood—particularly a door with true French windows—and you could easily pay $1000 or more, depending on the design.

TIP

Dont' use wood exterior sliders. Moisture will damage the wood and virtually every year you'll need to spend hours repainting or restaining.

The usual removal procedure is to lift out the slider. Yes, the door is heavy, so get help. Just slide it all the way open and then lift it off its track. To lift off the static portion of the slider, simply remove the two or three metal screws that are holding it in place. Then lift off the metal jamb by unscrewing it from the studs on the sides and the header above.

Remember that changing the slider means replacing an exterior door. Usually removal of the old door will involve some damage to the exterior facing and the interior drywall. If you're careful, however, you can limit the damage to less than an inch around the opening.

If you are installing another slider, you simply reverse the process. Afterward, you will probably need to do some repair work both inside and out. If you are replacing the slider with a wooden door, follow the procedures described above. The trim or molding that comes with the new door will often cover all or most of the damage done when removing the original slider.

Some vinyl sliders come with overlapping strips on the exterior. If you're careful, they can cover the outer wall damage incurred when removing the old slider.

21
Tips
When Painting

Painting should be the last job, after everything else is finished. You should first clean up, being sure to get rid of all dirt and dust. Only then should you start painting. In many renovations, even if you hire everything else out, you'll do the painting yourself. There's nothing wrong with this, but a few tips can help.

How Do I Remove Old Paint?

You may not need to take off the old paint. If the old surface is in good shape, all you may need to do is to remove any loose, flaky paint. Usually a paint scraper, available at any hardware store, will do the job. If you remove some chips of paint, sand the surface to make it uniform before painting. (If there are low spots or holes, you will want to caulk these before sanding.)

On the other hand, sometimes the existing paint is simply thick with old layers; it's got wrinkles in it or "alligator" cracks. If that's the case, you'll need to remove it—and that can be a hassle.

Sandpaper, first coarse then light, should be your first approach. If it easily gets rid of the old problem paint, consider yourself lucky. If not, you need a harsher tactic—stripping. There are a variety of chemical strippers available. In my experience, all are messy and most are smelly and require gloves. Sometimes it's simpler just to go back and lean more heavily on that paint scraper.

If all else fails, you can use heat from a torch. This will lift or bubble many paints so that you can easily strip them off with a putty knife. But be careful not to burn the underlying surface—or yourself. Also, be sure not to leave any debris lying around, since it could easily catch fire.

TRAP

Be wary of heat-stripping paint from an older house. Prior to 1978, lead was a common additive in paint. When you heat or burn lead-base paint, the lead can be released into the atmosphere. Inhale enough of it, and you or others could get lead poisoning—a deadly serious illness. Also beware of breathing in the dust created when sanding old paint.

What about Preparing the Surface?

All paint cans will tell you about their warranty, and one thing they inevitably say is that the warranty is valid only if the surface is properly prepared. That means you've sanded and filled to produce a smooth surface; then you primed that surface with a primer designed to work with the paint you have. Only now are you ready to apply the paint.

Smoothing the surface requires applying some sort of filler. There are a great many available. One of my favorites for filling in small holes is a lightweight, white, creamlike spackle found under many brand names. It is ready to use out of the container, will not expand or contract when it dries, and is easily paintable.

For grooves you will want a caulk that is squeezed from a tube, usually with a caulking gun. Latex caulks are the easiest to use, but be sure they are paintable. For sealing around wet areas, nothing is better than silicone caulk. It adheres tightly and almost never comes loose. However, often it cannot be painted, so you're stuck with the color that comes out.

What Types of Paints Are Available?

Needless to say, you can get paint in almost any color imaginable. But not all paints are available in all colors. Stains are generally available only in earth tones and may be either opaque, transparent, or semitransparent.

TIP

When painting over an already painted surface, use an oil-base paint over an oil-base paint, or acrylic latex over acrylic latex. Don't mix, or you'll get chipping.

Oil-base paints (also called alkyds) come in almost all colors and are extremely durable. However, they are smelly, require a thinner (petroleum solvent) to clean up, and take a long time to dry.

TRAP

Don't smoke when using oil-base paints, stains, or thinners. They are highly volatile and the fumes, in concentration, can explode.

Acrylic latex paints are synthetic and dry quickly (usually in less than an hour). Spots and spills can be cleaned up with water before the paint dries. (Once dried, acrylic latex cannot easily be removed.)

TIP

Finish what you begin as soon as possible when using acrylic latex paint. It dries very quickly and if you leave an area part painted and part unpainted, a visible line will show at the break.

Clear finishes include varnish, lacquer, and shellac. They are available either as polyurethane, a synthetic product, or as a natural "spar varnish." They are smelly and take a long time to dry. Use a thinner to clean up varnish and lacquer; use alcohol for shellac.

TIP

Buy paint in 5-gallon cans. The savings are enormous over buying five single-gallon cans. Just be sure you need all that paint!

Use only the best-quality paint. It will go on so much easier, whereas you'll have to fight with cheap paint. Also, it will "hide" better. "Hide" is the ability of the paint to prevent the undercoating from showing through. You'll know what I mean instantly if you've ever tried to apply white paint over a black surface. The black shows through, creating a gray result.

Good-quality paint has a better "hide" than cheap paint. Thus, while it may cost more initially, you'll save money by not having to put on so many coats. However, even a good-quality paint, if it's light, will require two coats over a darker surface to achieve a complete "hide."

What's the Best Way to Apply the Paint?

Brushes

You'll need to look into paint brushes, rollers, and sprayers—and possibly all three. Get several good-quality brushes. You'll appreciate it every time you take a stroke.

You need only three brushes: a large one (4") for covering large areas, a medium-size one (2½") for small areas, and a finish brush (1") for trim. If you carefully clean these brushes after each use, they will last you for years.

On high-quality brushes, bristles are flagged (of varying lengths) and split at the ends. When you check out a brush, make sure the bristles are soft and difficult, if not impossible, to pull out. You can also check out the quality of a brush by its price. Any time you pay more than $10 to $15 for a brush, you can be fairly sure it's a good one.

The most expensive brushes are those made with natural hog bristle. These are still the easiest to paint with.

TIP

Check for loose hairs on brushes before you start and remove them. If a hair comes off while you're painting, dab the end of the brush over the hair to pick it up.

Beware of cheap nylon (synthetic) brushes with bristles that aren't frayed at the ends and that are all of the same length. The paint will tend to drip off, and it will be difficult pulling the brush along a surface.

When painting with a brush, use long, steady strokes that are slightly overlapping. Be careful not to go over the same area more than once or twice; otherwise you'll start to get paint ridges. Try to work from one edge toward another, not from the middle out.

Rollers

When rollers came out more than 40 years ago, they were initially rejected by professional painters. Today everyone uses them for their speed and ease of application.

Be sure to buy a roller that's recommended for the type of paint you're using and for the surface you'll be rolling over. Generally speaking, short-nap rollers are used inside on smooth walls. Long-nap rollers are used outside on surfaces such as rough wood and stucco. Pay the extra cost for a good roller. The nap won't come off while you're painting and it won't drip paint.

You may also want to use paint pads. These are flat absorbent pads that can be used to get paint into otherwise hard-to-reach areas.

TIP

 When using a roller, apply the paint diagonally first, then finish up with top-to-bottom strokes (on a wall) or perpendicular strokes (on a ceiling). Be careful not to overroll the area, since it may cause the surface you are painting to come up. Paint from one edge toward another.

TRAP

 Don't try to get into corners and other hard-to-reach areas with a roller. Use a paint pad or brush. Never paint with a roller alone.

Sprayers

Paint sprayers are great for large areas, particularly those that have ornate work or unlevel surfaces. Sprayers work better outdoors than in.

Be aware that when you use a sprayer, the paint tends to spread everywhere, no matter how careful you are. For that reason, when painting inside, be sure to mask off *all* areas that you don't want sprayed. If necessary, hang plastic drop cloths to shield whole sections of a room. When painting outside, use drop cloths on the ground to protect plants and lawns. And *never* paint outside on a windy day, unless you want to pay for repainting your neighbor's car or house!

TRAP

When painting inside, always provide good ventilation. Paint fumes can sicken you, sometimes with permanent damage. They most often attack the lungs, kidneys, and brain and, hence, are nothing to fool around with.

TIP

If you're going to use more than one can of paint for a room, mix all the cans of paint together before starting. That way you'll get a uniform color.

What Are the Most Common Paint Problems?

There are a number of pitfalls to watch out for when you paint.

Bleeding. Bleeding usually occurs on exterior surfaces when a stain already on the surface bleeds through the new paint. Inside, too, problems can arise, as when children use crayons or permanent ink on walls. You may paint the area a dozen times, but the marks always bleed through. (Try spraying them with shellac first.)

Blistering.   Blistering occurs when you paint over a surface that is wet. For example, when you are painting outdoors over rotted wood or on a misty day, the moisture gets underneath the surface of the paint and lifts it up. Blistering usually occurs soon after painting. Be sure the surface is dry before you paint.

Chalking and Fading.   Chalking and fading may simply be the result of the aging process of the paint. If it's excessive, however, it could indicate an underlying water problem. The subsurface could be wet. You will need to dig down into the subsurface to determine where the moisture is coming from and then put up a barrier.

Nail Popping.   This occurs most often on sheet rock where the nail pops up, causing a protrusion in the paint, although it can occur on any surface. It might simply be that the nail was never properly hammered down. However, if rust marks show through, there is moisture in the wood from which the nail protrudes. You will probably have to get into the wall to determine where the moisture is coming from and then resolve the problem.

Wrinkling.   Wrinkling is usually an outdoor problem caused by putting on too much paint or painting on a hot day. Wrinkling can also occur if the previous coat (or primer) was not completely dry. Whatever the cause, you will need to strip the paint off and start over—a good reason to be extra careful!

TIP

 Paint will get on you no matter how careful you try to be. Rub on a lotion or petroleum jelly before you start. It will help keep the paint from sticking and make cleanup easier.

What's the Proper Order for Painting Interiors?

Of course, the question is what do you paint first, after all other work is done and everything is cleaned up and dust removed. The obvious answer is that you begin by painting that which is higher and which can drip down, such as the ceiling. The trouble is that obvious answers aren't always right.

It all depends on your plans for the trim. If you're going to be painting your trim (with latex or oil-base paint), then the proper order is as follows:

When Painting Trim

1. Paint ceiling

2. Paint walls

3. Paint doors and windows

4. Paint trim around doors, windows, and baseboards.

If, however, you're going to be staining your trim, then a different plan of action is in order. It looks like this:

When Staining Trim

1. Stain all trim, preferably before installing it. Use sanding sealer to raise the grain; then sand and varnish the trim.

2. If trim is already in place, stain as above, allow the stain to dry, and mask the trim.

3. Paint ceiling

4. Paint walls

5. Paint doors and windows

6. When all the paint is dry, either put in trim or remove masking from existing trim and touch up as necessary.

Remember that, if you get paint on the trim, you will have to sand it carefully—a tedious job—before you can restain it. Therefore, you want to do the painting and the staining separately.

What's the Proper Procedure for Painting Doors and Windows?

For doors, start at a top corner and work your way across and down. Use a brush and be sure that you work quickly to avoid having the paint dry. It's much harder to paint a glossy acrylic latex on a door than a glossy oil paint.

TRAP

Beware of backpainting a door with acrylic latex. This common practice involves painting the entire door with a roller, then using a brush to smooth out the paint and give it "brush marks." The problem is that acrylic latex dries quickly and unless you work fast, the bottom of the door (the last place you'll be working) will be dry before you get to it, leaving brush or roller marks.

For windows, particularly French windows (with lots of small panes of glass), painting can be a real hassle. You'll need to use a small (1-inch) trim brush for the dividers. You can try masking the glass, but that will take longer than the actual painting. Instead, use a plastic putty knife, found in paint stores, as a shield. Hold it against the surface you are painting to keep the paint away from the glass.

If you use a shield, you'll have to clean it off with a rag after each use, else some paint will get behind it and onto subsequent panes. Usually a little paint won't hurt. You can clean it off quickly with a rag, or come back later on and remove it with a razor blade. Beware of window glass that has a rough surface. It will be almost impossible to remove any dried paint from the glass.

TIP

Wear eye protection when painting. Getting a drop of paint in the eye, particularly oil-base paint, can be very painful and could damage the eye.

22
Adding a Deck

A deck adds more living space to your home. It combines the outdoors with the indoors. And, if properly designed and built, it can enhance the design of the property.

Adding a deck, however, is usually a poor investment in terms of getting back all the money when you resell. Indeed, as noted in Chapter 1, a deck can be expected to return only about a third of the money you invest.

Still, a deck adds enormously to the livability of a home. And, if you have dead area in the back (or front) of your home, you may need a deck simply to make the property more salable (in the same way you need a heating system).

Where Should the Deck Go?

You may be lucky and not have to decide on a location. An open area right at the back of your home may be naturally suited to a deck. On the other hand, perhaps the right spot is not so obvious. Your options may include the side yards as well.

When deciding on the location of the deck, try to imagine how it will change the appearance of the exterior of your home—for good—or for bad. Also, try to keep in mind what rooms you'll need to go through to get to it.

TIP

Look up when you're locating your deck. You don't want it where water or snow come off the roof.

Finally, think of what you'll use the deck for when planning its location. Many people like to barbecue on their decks, so easy access from the kitchen may be desirable. Also, children like to play on decks, so perhaps you'd like to be able to see what's going on out there. That means access from your family room, where you spend a lot of time, would be desirable.

How Big Should I Make the Deck?

Again, the size of the deck depends on what you want to use it for, and there are certain rules to keep in mind. If your deck is going to serve as a walkway, either out the back or into the front of the home, you'll want to leave an area at least 4 feet wide for access. If you're going to have a barbecue, you'll need at least 6 or 7 feet of space. If you're going to add an umbrella with chairs, you'll want 10 or 12 feet.

Be sure to consider appearance along with size. A huge deck on a small house will seem awkward, as will a small deck on a huge house. Try to match the deck to the home and the landscaping.

TIP

Decks are cheap, when compared with the cost of building a home. You might pay only a tenth as much for a deck as for additional interior space. Therefore, don't scrimp. Build the deck as large as is appropriate.

TRAP

If your deck is more than a few feet off the ground, your building department will require that you put a safety railing around it. Usually the railing must be at least 3 feet high, with no openings larger than 5 or 6 inches (so small children can't slip through). Check your local building code for the exact requirements in your area.

What Materials Should I Use to Build the Deck?

These days, you have a wide variety of choices. Usually the supports for the deck should be made from a sturdy wood—such as Douglas fir, hemlock, larch, and certain pines. Check to see what's available in your area. Look for wood that's been pressure-treated to reduce pests and rotting.

For the deck surface and railings, your first consideration should be durability. Remember, your deck will need to withstand heat and sunlight in summer, and rain, wind, and possibly snow in winter. Redwood is probably the best of the natural woods, followed by cedar. However, most of the redwood forests have been cut down, and good redwood is both hard to find and expensive. Heart wood (without knots) is difficult to come by at any price.

TRAP

Be way of using pressure-treated wood on the deck surfaces. The toxic chemicals that remain in the wood could pose a health hazard, particularly for children. For example, a simple splinter or sliver could introduce toxins into the blood system. For this reason, you may want to consider natural woods for all deck surfaces (although they have their own natural toxins!).

An alternative to wood is a type of fiberglass that comes in 2 × 4 and 2 × 6 sizes. It can be painted or stained to look like wood, and it holds up almost forever. Also, as wood prices increase, its price compares more and more favorably.

How Are Decks Constructed?

In a sense, decks are constructed much like houses. First there is a foundation, then framing, and then a top. However, whereas a house has a peripheral foundation running around the edges, a typical deck has only concrete footings with wooden posts on top.

The footings are usually poured concrete. In simplest form, they are created by digging a hole and then putting a form (often a hollow tube) into it. The concrete is then poured, and rebar is used for added strength.

A metal bracket is bolted to the top of the concrete to provide a more solid footing and to keep moisture (and termites) from traveling up into the wood and rotting it. The wood posts form the basic supports of the deck. Joists are laid across them at regular intervals (such as 16 or 24 inches), and the surface decking is placed on top.

A deck must be engineered. That means that the size of the posts and joists and the distances between them must be sufficient to ensure that the deck will hold a minimum amount of weight (usually 40 pounds per square foot) without collapsing.

However, a variety of books offer "preengineered" deck designs for you to follow. Further, since decks are so often do-it-yourself projects, many building departments will have sketches showing the basic structure and requirements.

TRAP

If your deck is more than 18 inches off the ground, you'll probably need a permit. If it is closer than that, you probably won't. However, check with your local building department to be sure. If you do need a permit, you can usually get one by supplying a rough sketch of the deck along with a sheet describing the type of wood and its size. (Plus, of course, the fee!)

Special Pointers When Building a Deck

A deck is often the first do-it-yourself project that homeowners undertake. It is not hard to build one, although hauling the lumber and concrete can be heavy work. Most decks are logically constructed. You needn't be a rocket scientist to figure them out. What you do need is patience and a little skill. Take the time to make sure that everything fits. Keep these special points in mind.

TIP

To ensure your deck's longevity, use long brass or galvanized screws to hold the deck surface down. The screws will keep the boards from popping up later on, and they won't leave rust marks.

Faceplate (Ledger).   If you're going to attach one side of a deck to a house, use a wooden faceplate bolted into the studs or the foundation of the house. Be sure the faceplate is at least 2 inches thick and as wide as the joists attaching to it.

Joist Hangers.   Some building departments require the use of joist hangers for decks. These metal holders, available at hardware stores in a wide variety of sizes and shapes, are a quick and sturdy way to attach joists. Be aware, however, that most commercially available joist hangers are not well galvanized and will rust out after 15 or 20 years.

Footings.   Be sure the footings are deep enough. In cold weather country, that means below the frost line. They must also extend upward above grade, typically 8 inches.

Sealers.   All wooden decks should be sealed with a preservative. However, many preservatives contain toxic chemicals, and some work better than others. Also, some building departments will not allow the use of certain preservatives—check first.

Sturdiness. The most common complaint about a deck is that it doesn't appear sturdy. Either the deck sags or it gives (is springy). To avoid sagging, be sure to pour the footings deep enough that they don't sink with the weight of the deck and people on it. To avoid springiness, make sure the joists are large enough for the deck and are laid out at appropriate intervals (not too wide a span).

When all is said and done, the final product—a finished deck—will add a dimension of livability and years of enjoyment to your home.

23

Adding a Garden Window

A garden window (sometimes called a box window) extends the window area about a foot outward from the house. It makes the room it's in look larger and more spacious. It also adds a certain elegance to the house.

Will you recoup the money you spend adding a garden window? The addition will likely cost between $500 and $1000, but it's hard to say whether your property will increase by that amount as a result. Certainly, adding the window will make your home more livable while you're in it and more salable later on.

Where Should I Add the Garden Window?

The easiest place to add a garden window is where a regular window already exists—particularly if the existing window and the new window are about the same size.

The advantage here is that you've already got the framing for the window. Demolition work can be held to a minimum. You may find that all you need to remove is some of the exterior skin of the home and a bit of the drywall inside. As a result, the patching required after installation will also be minimal. On the other hand, you may discover that there is no existing window where you want to place your garden window. Or the existing window is too small. (It's much easier if it's too large!)

If the window area is too small, you'll need to remove part of the wall where the new window is to go and then frame it. Begin by tearing out the existing studs. Next, put in a header of appropriate size (a heavy beam over the window that helps carry the weight of the roof formerly borne by the studs) and box the window area. The framing itself is neither difficult nor complicated; you can do it yourself or call in a carpenter or handyperson. In the process, however, you'll end up needing to repair the entire wall area both inside and out.

Do I Need Permits or Approval?

Check with your homeowners association, if you have one, since the work you're doing will extend the living area outward and will change the appearance of your home. In a condo situation, you will definitely need approval.

Further, if you're going to reframe the window area, you'll definitely need a permit from your local building department. On the other hand, if you're simply replacing one window with another of the same overall dimensions, a permit may not be required.

TIP

Any time you use glass in an area where it might be broken, the building code requires it to be safety glass (either tempered or laminated). These areas include skylights, bathrooms, and living areas where the window is below knee height (and someone might accidentally kick it). Garden windows do not usually fit into this class. However, moving plants into and out of a garden window can pose a danger to the glass. You may want to consider using safety glass, despite its higher cost.

What Type of Window Should I Choose?

In extreme climate conditions (hot or cold), you want as much insulation as possible from a window. If you live in the North, you want to insulate against cold in the winter. If you live in the South, you want to keep out heat in the summer. Insulating windows will cut down substantially on your utility costs. Don't make the mistake of thinking that because a window is small compared with the overall wall area of the house, it doesn't count in terms of thermal loss. It does.

The first U.S. observation station in Antarctica had a small glass dome open to the elements to let in light and to allow those inside to see out. It took as much energy to heat the dome as it did to heat the entire station of more than a dozen men working beneath the ice. Similarly in a home, most of the heat conductivity (loss) will come by way of the windows.

Probably the most common form of window insulation is double-pane glass. The two panes have a dead air space in between that is hermetically sealed. This almost cuts in half the conductivity of single-pane glass. Triple-pane glass reduces conductivity even further. Adding an inert gas, such as argon, also helps. Inert gases are heavier than air, meaning that their molecules move slower, thus reducing conductivity.

However, because of the design of garden windows, the added weight of double- or triple-pane glass may make its use impractical and costly. One alternative is Low-E (low-emissivity), high-transmittance glass, which has a special coating to reduce heat conductivity. At the same time, almost all natural light is still able to come through.

Low-E glass is high tech and produces some amazing results. Whereas a single pane of glass has an R rating of 1, usually Low-E glass can have an R rating anywhere from 4 to 7 or more. Further, because the glass has just a coating, its weight is relatively unaffected. Except for the added cost, Low-E glass is probably the best choice for a garden window.

What Type of Frame Should I Choose?

You have all sorts of choices in terms of frames. They can be wood, polyvinyl chloride (PVC), steel, or aluminum. Important considerations are the amount of maintenance required and the thermal qualities of the frame. Again, you are looking for materials that have low (or poor) heat conductivity.

Wood is the traditional frame, but it may not serve well in a garden window. To get the required strength to hold the window, you may need to add bulk. In addition, wood is a high-maintenance product. It must be sealed and painted regularly. However, as a poor conductor of heat, wood offers good thermal properties.

PVC is a relatively new product. It is rarely used in garden windows because it tends to be flimsy. In order to provide the necessary strength, it must be bulked up, creating an unattractive appearance. Vinyl can be easily painted. On the other hand, it is a good conductor of heat; hence it has poor thermal qualities.

Steel may be used for its rigidity. However, it is heavy and has high heat conductivity.

Aluminum is usually the frame of choice. It is lightweight, sturdy, and virtually maintenance free. It can be anodized in a variety of metallic colors. But it too is a good conductor of heat, and hence has poor thermal properties. Sometimes thermal breaks (essentially dead air spaces) are installed right into the frame to reduce the gain or loss of heat.

What about Installation and Costs?

Installation of a garden window is fairly easy. There are just five steps if you're replacing an existing window with a garden window that is close in size.

1. Remove the existing window. The amount of work involved will depend on the type of window you have. With an aluminum window, you will need to remove some of the interior drywall around the window frame and then some of the stucco or other exterior wall. Typically the window is simply nailed in place with flanges on the exterior. Remove the nails and it just pops out. With a wooden window, the entire frame will need to be removed. Use a crowbar to carefully separate it from the rough opening behind.

2. Move the new garden window into place. Use shims, if necessary for small differences in size. Get help in positioning the window, since it's awkward to hold and can be heavy. Be sure to check that it's level. The last thing you want to do is install a window that's on an angle!

3. Nail the new window in place. It's probably a good idea to use screws, particularly on the top, for added strength.

4. Replace and patch any damage done to the exterior wall and interior walls.

5. Finish up. Some garden windows have glass on the bottom. Others are designed to have a countertop that extends outward. Finish out the countertop portion, if needed.

If you're having a window custom-built, expect to pay big bucks. A single garden window 5 feet wide by 3 feet tall could easily cost you $1000 or more. On the other hand, you can buy a ready-made garden window for a quarter to half that price at any one of the many home supply companies, such as HomeBase.

TIP

If you buy a ready-made garden window, be sure to check on its insulating qualities. The R rating should appear right on the product.

A garden window will add light and airiness to any room. It is one of the easiest and least expensive ways to "expand" your home.

Index

Note: The *f.* after a page number refers to a figure.

About the Author

Robert Irwin has built homes from the ground up as well as completed dozens of major renovation and remodeling projects. He is best known as a real estate broker and the author of the best-selling *Tips & Traps* real estate series. He serves as a consultant to lenders, investors, and brokers. With over 50 books, including *Buying a Home on the Internet* and *The Pocket Guide for Home Buyers*, Irwin is recognized as one of the most knowledgeable writers in the real estate field today.